the beach house cookbook

the beach house cookbook

barbara scott-goodman • photographs by rita maas

CHRONICLE BOOKS

SAN FRANCISCO

Library of Congress Cataloging-in-Publication Data available.

ISBN: 0-8118-4308-4

Manufactured in China.

Art Direction and Design: Barbara Scott-Goodman

Food Styling: Roscoe Betsill

Prop Styling: Barbara Fritz

Distributed in Canada by Raincoast Books

9050 Shaughnessy Street

Vancouver, British Columbia V6P 6E5

10 9 8 7 6 5 4 3 2 1

Chronicle Books LLC

85 Second Street

San Francisco, California 94105

www.chroniclebooks.com

for Lester, Zan, and Isabelle,
my beach buddies

contents

introduction

I love vacationing at the beach. Being near the ocean in the warm and balmy summer season creates an atmosphere of freedom and high spirits that always inspires me. These are special days when we all savor well-deserved time off from busy careers and school and enjoy casual, spontaneous get-togethers with our friends and families. I like to keep meals and menus just as carefree during this time. Whether I'm grilling fish for my husband and two teenage daughters or boiling lobsters for a Fourth of July crowd, ease and convenience keep my vacation mood glowing.

Because summer foods are absolutely the best of the year, preparing bursting-with-flavor meals is a breeze. Fruits and vegetables, at the peak of perfection, are abundantly available from farm stands, local markets, and—if I arrange my guest list wisely—the gardens of my generous friends. All year long, I look forward to my first plate of thickly sliced sun-ripened tomatoes drizzled with olive oil, and our first dinner of sweet corn on the cob shared with friends on the deck as the sun sets. At this time, a variety of the freshest seafood is also available and can be easily prepared for delicious dinners. The warm weather months are a perfect time for grilling. Fire up the coals, and soon smoky aromas beckon friends and neighbors eager to enjoy the goodness of foods cooked outdoors. Who could resist sizzling steaks hot off the grill with a melange of fresh herbs, or stacks of juicy burgers with chopped fresh tomatoes and basil from the garden? Summer desserts also speak of the season. Simple cakes, pies, cobblers, and crisps are easy to prepare and taste heavenly when made with the ripest, peak-of-flavor fruits and berries available. It's good to take advantage of this precious time and be a bit self-indulgent. Have a piece of cake with fresh berry sauce and a tall glass of iced mint tea while hanging out on the porch on a lazy summer afternoon.

The recipes in this book use the best and freshest ingredients one can find while staying at the beach. It's fun to invite friends over for a drink before dinner and serve a few finger foods like Low-Country Pickled Shrimp or Grilled Caponata. They're great with special cocktails such as Vodka, Lemonade & Mint Coolers or White Rum & Lime Sea Breezes. Simple and fresh-tasting seafood dishes such as Steamed Mussels in Tomato-Fennel Broth and Garlic Shrimp with Parsley & Basil Sauce are delicious to serve for casual dinners. Grilled Lamb Chops with Mint Pesto Sauce and Beach House Burgers cooked on the grill are delectable and easy to make. Vibrant summer salads range from Ceviche Salad with Avocados & Tomatoes to Radicchio, Red Cabbage & Apple Slaw. Not to be outdone, easy-to-prepare desserts, laced with the ripest fruits and berries available, explode on the tongue with real flavor. Try the Strawberry-Rhubarb Pie, Peach & Blueberry Cobbler, or one of my all-time favorites, the luscious Grilled Peaches with Red Wine Sauce. The key to enjoying cooking at the beach is flexibility. While the recipes take full advantage of the best and freshest ingredients available in the summertime, you can substitute ingredients that are easier for you to find and still have a delicious dish.

One thing I've learned from many summer beach stays is that a well-equipped kitchen saves you time when you're preparing meals. If you are renting a house, inquire about the cooking facilities before you arrive. If the kitchen is not well supplied, I recommend bringing a variety of good sharp knives, a large lobster pot, and a blender or food processor. And make sure the house has a grill in good condition along with grilling accoutrements. Other kitchen essentials include a corkscrew, bottle opener, can opener, tongs, and nutcrackers. You may also want to bring along some of your favorite oils and vinegars and any hard-to-find condiments or spices, since you won't want to spend time shopping and paying beach-town prices for them.

This book is designed for you to cook and entertain in a relaxed manner. After all, it's summer vacation and you should enjoy it to the fullest. With just a bit of planning and organization, you can go to the beach, walk barefoot along the shore, swim in the pool, go for a hike, or read in a hammock all day—and still prepare great meals with style. That's what living at the beach is all about.

appetizers & finger foods

low-country pickled shrimp • shrimp
fritters with ginger-soy dipping sauce •
marinated tuna with sesame-baked wontons •
spicy clam dip • handmade pita crisps •
really good clams casino • mini–crab
cakes with cherry tomato & corn salsa •
smoked salmon tartare with dill sauce •
smoked trout spread • herbed white bean
spread • grilled caponata • spicy grilled
chicken satay

weekend afternoons

and evenings at the beach are great times to have friends over for drinks, and I always like to have a few good appetizers and snacks on hand for these occasions. Whether it's a simple spread made with white beans or a more complex dish like Shrimp Fritters with Ginger-Soy Dipping Sauce or Mini–Crab Cakes with Cherry Tomato & Corn Salsa, these appetizers invite guests to relax and share food in an informal and most enjoyable way.

All of the appetizers and finger foods in this chapter are terrific on their own or together in any combination for a larger cocktail party buffet. The only rule is to do what best fits your time frame and your mood.

low-country pickled shrimp

Inspired by the Low-Country cooking of South Carolina, this is excellent for serving with drinks before dinner or as part of a cocktail party buffet. The shrimp can be made well ahead of time since they need to marinate for a day or two. They are also very good when tossed into a salad of fresh greens and tomatoes.

SERVES 6

1 CUP TARRAGON VINEGAR

6 SLICES FRESH GINGER

2 TABLESPOONS CORIANDER SEEDS

1 TABLESPOON FENNEL SEEDS

1 TABLESPOON MIXED PEPPERCORNS

2½ POUNDS LARGE SHRIMP
   (ABOUT 32 TO 36 PER POUND)

1 MEDIUM RED ONION, THINLY SLICED

1 MEDIUM LEMON, THINLY SLICED

¼ CUP CAPERS, DRAINED

3 CLOVES GARLIC, THINLY SLICED

PINCH OF CAYENNE PEPPER

4 BAY LEAVES

¾ CUP EXTRA-VIRGIN OLIVE OIL

KOSHER SALT AND FRESHLY GROUND
   BLACK PEPPER

1. In a medium nonreactive saucepan, combine the vinegar, ½ cup of water, ginger, coriander and fennel seeds, and peppercorns. Bring to a boil over medium-high heat. Lower the heat and simmer for 10 minutes. Set the pickling mixture aside and let cool completely.

2. Bring a large pot of salted water to a boil. Add the shrimp. Remove from the heat and let stand until the shrimp turn pink, about 3 minutes. Drain, rinse, and let cool completely; then shell and devein the shrimp.

3. Put the shrimp in a large glass or ceramic bowl with the onion, lemon, capers, garlic, cayenne pepper, and bay leaves and gently toss together. Whisk the olive oil and salt and pepper to taste into the pickling mixture and pour over the shrimp. Cover tightly with plastic wrap and refrigerate for at least 24 hours or up to 3 days.

4. To serve the shrimp, remove them with a slotted spoon, transfer to a platter, and serve cold or at room temperature with toothpicks.

shrimp fritters with ginger-soy dipping sauce

I like to serve these shrimp fritters with cocktails. They are made with fresh shrimp dipped in a batter of white and chickpea flours, then quickly fried in hot oil. You can't make too many of these—they are crispy, crunchy, and utterly delicious.

SERVES 6; MAKES ABOUT 3 DOZEN FRITTERS

½ CUP UNBLEACHED WHITE FLOUR

½ CUP CHICKPEA FLOUR

I TABLESPOON KOSHER SALT

½ POUND MEDIUM SHRIMP (ABOUT 18),
    SHELLED, DEVEINED, AND FINELY CHOPPED

¼ CUP CHOPPED ONION

¼ CUP CHOPPED FRESH FLAT-LEAF PARSLEY

CANOLA OR SAFFLOWER OIL FOR FRYING

GINGER-SOY DIPPING SAUCE:

½ CUP LOW-SODIUM SOY SAUCE

2 TABLESPOONS RICE VINEGAR

2 TABLESPOONS SUGAR

I TABLESPOON MINCED FRESH GINGER

2 TABLESPOONS MINCED SCALLIONS

DASH OF HOT SAUCE

1. In a large bowl, whisk the flours with the salt and gradually whisk in 1 cup of water until smooth. Stir in the shrimp, onion, and parsley. (The batter can be made up to 3 hours ahead of time and kept in the refrigerator.)

2. To make the Dipping Sauce, whisk together the soy sauce, vinegar, sugar, ginger, scallions, and hot sauce. Pour into small bowls and set aside until ready to serve.

3. Pour the oil into a large skillet to a depth of ¼ inch and heat over high heat. Drop the batter by teaspoonfuls into the oil. Fry until just golden underneath, about 2 minutes. Turn and fry on the other side. Drain on paper towels and serve at once with the Dipping Sauce.

marinated tuna with sesame-baked wontons

Here is a really easy appetizer to prepare using sushi-quality tuna, which is the freshest and best you can buy. Let the tuna slices mellow in a sake-based marinade for a short time, 2 hours tops, and serve them on wontons that have been quickly baked with a dash of sesame oil.

SERVES 4 TO 6; MAKES ABOUT 30 TUNA-TOPPED WONTONS

1½ TABLESPOONS LOW-SODIUM SOY SAUCE	SESAME OIL FOR BRUSHING
2 TABLESPOONS SAKE	15 WONTON WRAPPERS (SEE NOTE)
2 TABLESPOONS BROWN SUGAR	6 SCALLIONS, TRIMMED AND MINCED,
1 TABLESPOON FRESH LEMON JUICE	FOR GARNISH
¾ POUND SUSHI-QUALITY TUNA	SESAME SEEDS FOR GARNISH

1. In a small bowl, whisk the soy sauce, sake, sugar, and lemon juice together. Pour a bit of the mixture into a nonreactive baking dish to cover the bottom.
2. Using a very sharp knife, cut the tuna into ¼-inch-thick pieces, about 1 inch long. Arrange the tuna in the baking dish in one layer and pour the remaining marinade over them. Cover and refrigerate for 1½ to 2 hours, but no longer.
3. Preheat the oven to 350°F. Brush a baking sheet with sesame oil.
4. Cut the wonton wrappers in half, on the diagonal, to make triangles. Place them on the baking sheet and lightly brush with a bit more oil. Bake until just lightly browned and crisp, 4 to 5 minutes. Remove from the oven and set aside to cool a bit.
5. Place a piece of tuna on each baked wonton, garnish with scallions and sesame seeds, and serve at once.

Note: Wonton wrappers are available at Asian markets, health food stores, and gourmet supermarkets.

spicy clam dip

Everyone loves this easy-to-make, zesty clam dip. Prepare it ahead of time and serve slightly chilled with pita crisps and garden-fresh vegetables. It's also very good stuffed into celery and topped with chopped black olives.

SERVES 8; MAKES ABOUT 1½ CUPS

12 CHERRYSTONE CLAMS, SCRUBBED
  AND RINSED
1 PACKAGE (½ POUND) CREAM CHEESE,
  AT ROOM TEMPERATURE
½ CUP LOW-FAT SOUR CREAM

½ MEDIUM RED BELL PEPPER, STEMMED,
  SEEDED, AND FINELY DICED
1 TEASPOON CELERY SEED
1 TO 2 TEASPOONS HOT SAUCE
KOSHER SALT

1. Put the clams in a large soup pot, add 2 cups of water, and bring to a boil. Cover and cook until the clams open, about 5 minutes. (Discard any that do not open.) Drain and let cool. When cool enough to handle, remove the clams from their shells, coarsely chop, and set aside.

2. Put the clams, cream cheese, sour cream, bell pepper, celery seed, hot sauce, and salt to taste in a food processor. Process in short pulses until fine, but not too smooth. Taste and adjust the seasonings, if necessary, and process again briefly. Scrape the dip into a bowl, cover, and chill. The dip will keep in the refrigerator for up to 3 days.

handmade pita crisps

These pita crisps are terrific for serving with all kinds of dips, spreads, and salsas. They are also very good served with Grilled Caponata (page 29).

MAKES ABOUT 12 DOZEN CRISPS

¾ CUP OLIVE OIL

2 TEASPOONS PAPRIKA

TEN 6-INCH PITA POCKETS

KOSHER SALT

1. Preheat the oven to 350°F.
2. In a small bowl, stir together the olive oil and paprika.
3. Using a sharp knife, halve each pita so that you have 2 circles and no pocket. Brush the rough sides of the pitas with the paprika oil and season generously with salt to taste.
4. Cut each pita half into 7 or 8 wedges and arrange them in single layers on large, ungreased baking sheets. Bake in the middle of the oven until lightly browned and crisp, about 10 minutes. Cool on wire racks before serving. The pita crisps can be made up to 2 days ahead of time and stored in resealable plastic bags at room temperature.

really good clams casino

Clams casino, or stuffed clams, have long been an appetizer staple on seafood menus. The clams, and not the bread crumbs, should be the main ingredient in this dish, but this is often not the case. My updated version of clams casino includes shallots, scallions, fresh herbs, and chopped fresh cherrystone clams. They are "really good."

SERVES 6; MAKES 18 STUFFED CLAMS

18 CHERRYSTONE CLAMS, SCRUBBED
AND RINSED

3 CUPS DRY WHITE WINE

2 SLICES BACON

2 TABLESPOONS UNSALTED BUTTER

1 CLOVE GARLIC, MINCED

3 TABLESPOONS FINELY CHOPPED SHALLOTS

4 SCALLIONS, TRIMMED AND MINCED

1/2 CUP FINELY CHOPPED FRESH
FLAT-LEAF PARSLEY

2 TABLESPOONS FINELY CHOPPED
FRESH BASIL

1/2 MEDIUM RED BELL PEPPER, STEMMED,
SEEDED, AND FINELY DICED

1/4 CUP PLAIN DRY BREAD CRUMBS

1/4 TEASPOON RED PEPPER FLAKES

SALT AND FRESHLY GROUND BLACK PEPPER

2 TO 3 TABLESPOONS EXTRA-VIRGIN OLIVE OIL

2 TO 3 TABLESPOONS FRESHLY GRATED
PARMESAN CHEESE (OPTIONAL)

LEMON WEDGES FOR SERVING

HOT SAUCE FOR SERVING

1. Put the clams in a large soup pot, add the wine, and bring to a boil. Cover and cook until the clams begin to open. Remove the clams from the pot with a slotted spoon as they open and transfer to a colander. (Discard any that do not open.) Drain and let cool. When cool enough to handle, remove the clams from their shells and reserve 18 shells for stuffing. Finely chop the clams and set aside.

2. Preheat the oven to 425°F.

3. In a large skillet, cook the bacon until crisp. Transfer to a plate lined with paper towels. Drain all but 1 tablespoon of bacon fat. Over medium heat, add the butter to the pan and cook until melted. Add the garlic, shallots, scallions, parsley, basil, and bell pepper and cook until softened, about 5 minutes, stirring well. Add the chopped clams and cook for about 2 minutes. Turn down the heat to very low, add the bread crumbs, red pepper flakes, and salt and pepper to taste and mix well to combine. Crumble the bacon and add to the mixture. Add a bit of white wine or water if the mixture seems too dry. Remove from the heat.

4. With a large spoon, stuff the mixture into the reserved clam shells. Arrange the stuffed clams on a baking sheet and drizzle with the olive oil. Sprinkle the clams with the cheese, if desired.

5. Bake the clams until the tops are lightly browned, about 10 minutes. Serve at once with lemon wedges and hot sauce.

mini-crab cakes with cherry tomato & corn salsa

It's all too easy to find bad crab cakes. I prefer crab cakes that are mostly crab and very little breading. After testing and trying many combinations of crab, bread crumbs, and mayonnaise, I finally found the right mix of ingredients for a great-tasting crab cake. It is necessary to refrigerate them for at least an hour before cooking them so they don't fall apart. These crab cakes and salsa are served over salad greens, and make a wonderful first course for a seafood dinner.

SERVES 6; MAKES 18 CRAB CAKES

1 POUND LUMP CRABMEAT, PICKED OVER

1 TABLESPOON FRESH LEMON JUICE

1/2 CUP PLAIN DRY BREAD CRUMBS

1 LARGE EGG

1/4 CUP PLUS 1 TABLESPOON MAYONNAISE

2 SCALLIONS, TRIMMED AND MINCED

1 TABLESPOON CHOPPED FRESH
    FLAT-LEAF PARSLEY

1 TABLESPOON DRY MUSTARD

SALT AND FRESHLY GROUND BLACK PEPPER

2 TABLESPOONS UNSALTED BUTTER

2 TABLESPOONS CANOLA OR SAFFLOWER OIL

6 CUPS SALAD GREENS

CHERRY TOMATO & CORN SALSA
    (FACING PAGE)

1. Put the crabmeat in a medium bowl, sprinkle with the lemon juice, and gently toss.
2. In a large bowl, mix together the bread crumbs, egg, mayonnaise, scallions, parsley, mustard, and salt and pepper to taste. Add the crabmeat and mix together gently.
3. Shape into small patties, about 1 inch thick and 2 inches wide, and place on a baking sheet. Cover with plastic wrap and refrigerate for at least an hour.
4. Heat 1 tablespoon each of the butter and oil in a large skillet over medium-high heat and cook half of the crab cakes until golden, 3 to 5 minutes per side. Drain on paper towels. Heat the remaining butter and oil and repeat with the rest of the crab cakes.
5. To serve, divide the salad greens among 6 plates. Top each plate with 3 crab cakes and spoon the salsa over them.

cherry tomato & corn salsa

In addition to crab cakes, this salsa is delicious with corn chips or crudités.

MAKES ABOUT 3 CUPS

2 EARS FRESH CORN, HUSKED

2 CUPS CHERRY TOMATOES,
   COARSELY CHOPPED

1/2 MEDIUM RED ONION, FINELY DICED

2 SCALLIONS, TRIMMED AND MINCED

1 1/2 TABLESPOONS CAPERS, DRAINED

1 TABLESPOON BALSAMIC VINEGAR

1 TEASPOON GROUND CUMIN

1 TEASPOON HOT SAUCE, OR TO TASTE

1. Bring a large pot of water to a boil. Add the corn, return to the boil, and cook for 5 minutes. Lift the corn from the water and set aside to cool. When cool enough to handle, scrape the kernels off the cobs with a small, sharp knife and transfer to a large bowl.

2. Add the tomatoes, onion, scallions, capers, vinegar, cumin, and hot sauce and toss gently. Cover and refrigerate for at least 2 hours before serving. The salsa will keep in the refrigerator for up to 3 days.

smoked salmon tartare with dill sauce

Smoked salmon is always elegant to serve as an hors d'oeuvre. Here it is chopped and combined with red onion and capers and served with a smooth and tasty sauce laced with fresh dill. Serve on sliced pumpernickel, rye crackers, or, for a real treat, toasted challah bread.

SERVES 6 TO 8; MAKES ABOUT 2 DOZEN TOASTS

½ POUND SMOKED SALMON,
    COARSELY CHOPPED
3 TABLESPOONS FINELY CHOPPED RED ONION
1½ TABLESPOONS CAPERS, DRAINED
3 TABLESPOONS FRESH LEMON JUICE
1½ TABLESPOONS EXTRA-VIRGIN OLIVE OIL
FRESHLY GROUND BLACK PEPPER

DILL SAUCE:
½ CUP MAYONNAISE
2 TEASPOONS DIJON MUSTARD
2 TABLESPOONS CHOPPED FRESH DILL
2 TEASPOONS WHOLE MILK
PINCH OF SUGAR

SLICED PUMPERNICKEL BREAD, TOASTED CHALLAH
    BREAD, OR RYE CRACKERS FOR SERVING
DILL SPRIGS FOR GARNISH

1. Combine the salmon, onion, capers, lemon juice, olive oil, and pepper to taste in a medium bowl and mix together gently.
2. To make the Dill Sauce, combine the mayonnaise, mustard, and dill in a small bowl and mix together. Add the milk and sugar and mix again. Taste and adjust the seasonings, if necessary.
3. To serve, spread a bit of the Dill Sauce over the pumpernickel, challah toast, or cracker, top with a spoonful of the tartare, and garnish with a dill sprig.

smoked trout spread

Living at the beach should always be easy and casual, and there's nothing simpler than making this spread. It's delicate, smooth, and smoky—just the right thing to serve to friends dropping by for a drink on a summer night.

SERVES 6; MAKES ABOUT 1 1/2 CUPS

3/4 CUP WHOLE-MILK RICOTTA CHEESE

1/4 CUP LOW-FAT SOUR CREAM

1/2 POUND SMOKED TROUT FILLET,
   CUT INTO SMALL PIECES (SEE NOTE)

1 TABLESPOON PREPARED HORSERADISH,
   DRAINED

2 SCALLIONS, TRIMMED AND MINCED

2 TABLESPOONS CHOPPED FRESH DILL

1 TEASPOON FRESH LEMON JUICE

FRESHLY GROUND BLACK PEPPER

Combine the ricotta cheese, sour cream, smoked trout, horseradish, scallions, dill, lemon juice, and pepper to taste in a food processor. Process until smooth. Taste and adjust the seasonings, if necessary, and process again. Scrape into a bowl, cover, and chill in the refrigerator 2 to 3 hours before serving. Serve with bread, toasts, or crackers.

Note: Smoked trout is available in fish markets and specialty markets where high-quality smoked fish is sold.

herbed white bean spread

This is a fantastic spread to serve over grilled bread and top with an array of delicious things, such as roasted red and yellow bell pepper strips, pimientos or piquillo peppers, black and green olives, anchovies, and caramelized onions. On its own, the spread is delicious, but the toppings really make it something special.

SERVES 6; MAKES ABOUT 1 ½ CUPS

2 TABLESPOONS OLIVE OIL

4 CLOVES GARLIC, HALVED

1 SMALL RED ONION, CHOPPED

1 CAN (15.5 OUNCES) CANNELLINI BEANS,
    RINSED AND DRAINED

2 TABLESPOONS CHOPPED FRESH
    FLAT-LEAF PARSLEY

1 TABLESPOON CHOPPED FRESH BASIL

1 TEASPOON CHOPPED FRESH CHIVES

1 TEASPOON CHOPPED FRESH THYME

2 TABLESPOONS FRESH LEMON JUICE

1 TABLESPOON CRÈME FRAÎCHE
    OR SOUR CREAM

SALT AND FRESHLY GROUND BLACK PEPPER

GRILLED BREAD, TOASTS, OR CRACKERS
    FOR SERVING

ROASTED RED OR YELLOW BELL PEPPERS,
    PIMIENTOS, PIQUILLO PEPPERS, BLACK OLIVES,
    GREEN OLIVES, ANCHOVIES, CARAMELIZED
    ONIONS, AND CAPERS FOR GARNISH

1. Heat the olive oil in a large sauté pan and cook the garlic and onion over medium heat until softened and golden, about 10 minutes. Add the beans, parsley, basil, chives, thyme, and 1 tablespoon of the lemon juice and cook over medium heat, stirring occasionally, until the beans are cooked through, about 10 minutes.

2. When cool enough to handle, transfer the bean mixture to a food processor. Add the crème fraîche or sour cream and process until smooth. Add the remaining tablespoon of lemon juice, season to taste with salt and pepper, and process again until smooth.

3. Serve at room temperature over grilled bread, toasts, or crackers and top with desired garnishes.

grilled caponata

Caponata is usually made by roasting or sautéing eggplants and onions, but recently I cooked them on the grill. The nicely charred and smoky vegetables mixed with tomatoes, capers, and olives tasted wonderful. I highly recommend making this version in the warm weather months when the grill is handy. Caponata is great to serve as an hors d'oeuvre with Handmade Pita Crisps, and it's also very good with grilled lamb.

SERVES 12; MAKES ABOUT 6 CUPS

3 MEDIUM EGGPLANTS, PEELED AND CUT
    INTO 1/2-INCH-THICK SLICES

2 LARGE RED ONIONS, CUT INTO
    1/2-INCH-THICK SLICES

1/2 CUP OLIVE OIL FOR BRUSHING

1/2 CUP GOLDEN RAISINS

3/4 CUP RED WINE

1 CAN (28 OUNCES) PLUM TOMATOES,
    COARSELY CHOPPED, JUICE RESERVED

3 TABLESPOONS CAPERS, DRAINED

1/2 CUP KALAMATA OLIVES, DRAINED,
    PITTED, AND CHOPPED

1/4 CUP BALSAMIC VINEGAR

1/2 CUP CHOPPED FRESH FLAT-LEAF PARSLEY

SALT AND FRESHLY GROUND BLACK PEPPER

HANDMADE PITA CRISPS (PAGE 19), CRACKERS,
    OR BREAD FOR SERVING

1. Preheat the oven to 400°F. Prepare a charcoal or gas grill. Let the coals heat until medium-hot, so they are covered with a light coating of ash and glow deep red.

2. Generously brush the eggplant and onion slices with olive oil and arrange on separate baking sheets. Roast in the oven, turning once, until soft, 10 to 15 minutes.

3. Transfer the eggplant and onions to the grill and cook until nicely browned, turning often, about 5 minutes total cooking time. Set aside to cool.

4. Put the raisins in a small saucepan and cover with the wine. Bring to a simmer over medium heat and cook for 3 minutes. Set aside to allow the raisins to plump.

continued

5. Put the tomatoes and their juice into a large mixing bowl. Stir in the raisins and wine, capers, olives, and vinegar. Chop the grilled eggplant and onions into small pieces and add to the tomato mixture. Toss well to combine.

   Add the parsley and salt and pepper to taste. Cover and let the mixture mellow for 6 to 8 hours or overnight in the refrigerator. The caponata will keep in the refrigerator, covered, for up to 1 week.

6. Before serving, taste and adjust the seasonings, if necessary. Serve at room temperature with pita crisps, crackers, or bread.

spicy grilled chicken satay

Satay, bite-sized cubes of meat grilled on skewers, is wonderful to serve as an hors d'oeuvre. Here chicken is marinated in a spicy peanut sauce and grilled over a medium-hot fire.

SERVES 6; MAKES 18 SKEWERS

2 TABLESPOONS SMOOTH PEANUT BUTTER

2 TABLESPOONS PLAIN LOW-FAT YOGURT

1½ TABLESPOONS LOW-SODIUM SOY SAUCE

1 TABLESPOON FRESH LIME JUICE

2 TEASPOONS MINCED FRESH GINGER

2 TEASPOONS SUGAR

PINCH OF RED PEPPER FLAKES

½ POUND SKINLESS, BONELESS CHICKEN
   BREASTS, CUT INTO 1-INCH CUBES

8 SCALLIONS, TRIMMED, FOR GARNISH

LIME WEDGES FOR GARNISH

1. Combine the peanut butter, yogurt, soy sauce, lime juice, ginger, sugar, and red pepper flakes in a blender and blend until smooth. Transfer to a medium bowl. Add the chicken and stir to coat completely. Cover and refrigerate for at least 1 hour or up to 6. Soak 18 bamboo skewers in cold water for at least 1 hour.

2. Prepare a charcoal or gas grill.

3. Remove the chicken from the marinade, but do not pat dry. Reserve the marinade. Thread 2 pieces of chicken onto each skewer.

4. When the fire is medium-hot, and the coals are covered with a light coating of ash and glow deep red, place the skewers around the outside of the grill so that the ends of the skewers are not exposed to direct heat. Grill the chicken, turning and basting with the marinade, until browned outside and white in the center, about 5 minutes.

5. Place the skewers on a large platter and garnish with scallions and lime wedges. Serve at once.

soups, chowders & sandwiches

farmers' market vegetable soup with pesto sauce • creamy carrot & chive soup • gazpacho with grilled shrimp & corn • tomato-basil soup with mussels • oyster & vegetable bisque • cool clam chowder • shellfish chowder • red clam chowder • lobster & corn chowder • chicken salad niçoise sandwiches • lobster rolls • shrimp burgers with chili mayonnaise • fried oyster rolls with spicy tartar sauce

soups and sandwiches are great fun to make and eat for casual, summertime meals. Vegetables and herbs from the garden and local farmstands are delightfully fresh, and a wide variety of fish and shellfish from local waters is readily available for creating all kinds of soups, bisques, and chowders. Whether it's gazpacho for lunch on a hot summer afternoon, or shellfish chowder on a rainy evening, these soups feed both the stomach and the soul.

Served with soup or on their own, the delicious sandwiches in this chapter, such as Chicken Salad Niçoise and Lobster Rolls, are easy to prepare and great for lunches, snacks, and picnics.

farmers' market vegetable soup with pesto sauce

This delicious, aromatic soup combines the best of late summer's harvest, when fresh tomatoes, zucchini, corn, and green beans are at their peak flavor. When making this soup, feel free to experiment with other farm-fresh vegetables—whatever looks best at the market.

SERVES 6

½ CUP DRIED GREAT NORTHERN BEANS

KOSHER SALT

2 TABLESPOONS OLIVE OIL

2 CLOVES GARLIC, THINLY SLICED

1 MEDIUM ONION, THINLY SLICED

2 MEDIUM CARROTS, PEELED AND DICED

2 CELERY RIBS, DICED

4 CUPS CHICKEN OR VEGETABLE BROTH,
    PREFERABLY HOMEMADE

2 LARGE RIPE TOMATOES,
    COARSELY CHOPPED, WITH THEIR JUICE

4 SMALL NEW POTATOES, CUT
    INTO ¼-INCH DICE

1 SMALL ZUCCHINI, PEELED AND CUT
    INTO ¼-INCH DICE

1 CUP FRESH CORN KERNELS
    (FROM 2 OR 3 LARGE EARS SWEET CORN)

1 CUP GREEN BEANS, TRIMMED AND CUT
    INTO 1-INCH PIECES

¼ CUP CHOPPED FRESH FLAT-LEAF PARSLEY

FRESHLY GROUND BLACK PEPPER

PESTO SAUCE:

1 CUP FRESH BASIL, RINSED AND DRIED

1 CLOVE GARLIC, SLICED

½ CUP WALNUTS

½ CUP EXTRA-VIRGIN OLIVE OIL

¼ CUP FRESHLY GRATED PARMESAN CHEESE

KOSHER SALT AND FRESHLY GROUND
    BLACK PEPPER

1. Put the beans in a bowl and add cold water to cover. Soak them for a few hours or overnight. Drain and put them in a large saucepan. Add water to cover, salt to taste and bring to a boil over high heat. Reduce the heat, cover, and simmer, stirring occasionally, until just tender, 50 to 60 minutes. Drain and set aside.

continued

2. Heat the olive oil in a large soup pot over medium-high heat. Add the garlic and onion and cook until softened, about 5 minutes. Add the carrots and celery, cover, and cook until tender, about 10 minutes.

3. Add the broth and 2 cups of water, bring to a boil, and reduce the heat to medium. Add the tomatoes, potatoes, and zucchini and simmer for about 20 minutes, stirring occasionally. Stir in the corn, green beans, and reserved white beans and cook for about 10 minutes. (The soup may be cooked up to this point and refrigerated until just before serving.)

4. To make the Pesto Sauce, put the basil, garlic, and walnuts in the bowl of a food processor and process to combine. With the motor running, add the olive oil in a slow, steady stream. Shut the motor off and add the cheese and salt and pepper to taste. Process briefly to combine and scrape into a bowl.

5. Just before serving the soup, add the parsley and season with salt and pepper. Ladle into soup bowls and add a generous spoonful of Pesto Sauce to each serving. Serve with additional Parmesan cheese, if desired.

creamy carrot & chive soup

Served hot or cold, this delicate, creamy soup, topped with a dollop of yogurt and sprinkled with fresh chives, makes an elegant starter for a lunch or dinner party.

SERVES 6

2 TABLESPOONS UNSALTED BUTTER

3 MEDIUM WHITE ONIONS, CHOPPED

3 CUPS CHICKEN BROTH, PREFERABLY
    HOMEMADE

6 LARGE CARROTS, PEELED AND DICED

2 LARGE RUSSET POTATOES, PEELED
    AND DICED

PINCH OF CAYENNE PEPPER

KOSHER SALT AND FRESHLY GROUND
    BLACK PEPPER

YOGURT-CHIVE CREAM:

1/4 CUP PLAIN LOW-FAT YOGURT

1/4 CUP LOW-FAT SOUR CREAM

2 TABLESPOONS MINCED FRESH CHIVES

FRESH CHIVES FOR GARNISH

1. Melt the butter in a large soup pot over medium heat and sauté the onions until softened, about 5 minutes.

2. Add the broth, 2 cups of water, the carrots, and potatoes. Bring to a boil, reduce the heat, and simmer, partially covered, until the vegetables are very tender, about 25 minutes. Remove the pot from the heat and let the soup cool.

3. Purée the soup in batches in a blender or food processor until very smooth. Return the soup to the pot. Season with the cayenne pepper and salt and pepper to taste.

4. To make the Yogurt-Chive Cream, mix the yogurt, sour cream, and chives together in a small bowl.

5. If serving warm, reheat the soup gently over low heat. If serving cold, chill in the refrigerator for at least 4 hours. Serve the soup garnished with a spoonful of the Yogurt-Chive Cream and a sprinkling of fresh chives.

gazpacho with grilled shrimp & corn

This version of gazpacho always wins raves from my guests. It is truly a summertime treat.

SERVES 6

4 MEDIUM TOMATOES, CORED AND CUT
INTO SMALL WEDGES

2 MEDIUM RED BELL PEPPERS, STEMMED,
SEEDED, AND FINELY CHOPPED

2 MEDIUM CUCUMBERS, PEELED, SEEDED,
AND COARSELY CHOPPED

1 MEDIUM RED ONION, COARSELY CHOPPED

2 CLOVES GARLIC, THINLY SLICED

2 CUPS CHICKEN BROTH, PREFERABLY
HOMEMADE

1/3 CUP SHERRY VINEGAR

DASH OF HOT SAUCE

PINCH OF CAYENNE PEPPER

2 TABLESPOONS CAPERS, DRAINED

KOSHER SALT AND FRESHLY GROUND
BLACK PEPPER

1/2 POUND LARGE SHRIMP (ABOUT 18),
PEELED AND DEVEINED

2 EARS FRESH CORN, HUSKED

OLIVE OIL FOR BRUSHING

1/4 CUP CHOPPED FRESH FLAT-LEAF PARSLEY
FOR GARNISH

1/4 CUP CHOPPED FRESH CILANTRO
FOR GARNISH

1. Combine the tomatoes, bell peppers, cucumbers, onion, garlic, broth, vinegar, hot sauce, cayenne pepper, capers, and salt and pepper to taste in a large bowl and stir to mix well.

2. Transfer half of the mixture to a blender or a food processor and process until smooth. Return to the bowl and mix well. Taste and adjust the seasonings, if necessary. Cover and refrigerate the soup for at least 4 hours, or overnight.

3. Prepare a charcoal or gas grill and let the coals heat until medium-hot, so they are covered with a light coating of ash and glow deep red. Brush the shrimp and corn with olive oil and grill, turning often, until cooked through, about 5 minutes. (A grill pan works well for this.)

4. When cool enough to handle, scrape the corn from the cobs with a small, sharp knife and add to the gazpacho.

5. Ladle the soup into chilled shallow soup bowls, top with the grilled shrimp, sprinkle with the parsley and cilantro, and serve at once.

tomato-basil soup with mussels

Delicious, light tomato soup, enhanced with cream and fresh basil, and spooned over freshly steamed mussels, is a good thing to serve when you're in the mood for a taste of the sea. The broth, made with canned plum tomatoes, can be made well ahead of time and refrigerated or frozen.

SERVES 4

2 TABLESPOONS UNSALTED BUTTER

1 MEDIUM ONION, THINLY SLICED

3 CLOVES GARLIC, THINLY SLICED

1 MEDIUM CARROT, PEELED AND CHOPPED

1 CAN (28 OUNCES) PLUM TOMATOES, COARSELY CHOPPED, JUICE RESERVED

PINCH OF SUGAR

KOSHER SALT AND FRESHLY GROUND BLACK PEPPER

¾ CUP LIGHT CREAM OR HALF-AND-HALF

8 FRESH BASIL LEAVES, THINLY SLICED

1½ POUNDS MUSSELS, SCRUBBED, DEBEARDED, AND RINSED

1. Melt the butter in a large soup pot over medium heat and sauté the onion, garlic, and carrot until the vegetables are softened, about 10 minutes.

2. Add the tomatoes and their juice, sugar, and salt and pepper to taste. Add 1 cup of water and slowly bring to a boil. Reduce the heat to low and simmer for 30 minutes. Remove the pot from the heat and let the soup cool.

3. Purée the soup, in batches, in a food processor until very smooth. (At this point, the soup may be refrigerated or frozen.) Return the soup to the pot and add the cream or half-and-half and basil. Taste and adjust the seasonings, if necessary, and heat through over very low heat.

4. Put the mussels in a large sauté pan and add 1 cup of water. Bring to a boil, cover the pan tightly, and cook until the mussels have opened, 3 to 5 minutes. (Discard any that do not open.)

5. To serve, place about 8 mussels in each of 4 large soup bowls and spoon the warm soup over them. Serve at once.

oyster & vegetable bisque

Because oysters are now readily available, we can savor these briny treats year-round. They add just the right touch to this creamy soup, making it a lovely starter or light main course. Whether you shuck the oysters yourself or have your fishmonger do it, be sure that the tasty oyster liquor is reserved. When making this soup, take care not to overcook the oysters. When their edges begin to curl, they are ready to eat.

SERVES 6

18 SMALL OYSTERS, IN THEIR SHELLS, SCRUBBED AND RINSED

2 TABLESPOONS UNSALTED BUTTER

6 SCALLIONS, TRIMMED AND MINCED

1 CUP THINLY SLICED SHIITAKE MUSHROOMS

3 MEDIUM CARROTS, PEELED AND CUT INTO JULIENNE ABOUT 1 INCH LONG

2 CUPS DRY WHITE WINE

1 CUP WHOLE MILK

2 CUPS HALF-AND-HALF

KOSHER SALT AND FRESHLY GROUND BLACK PEPPER

1 BUNCH WATERCRESS, STEMMED AND CHOPPED (ABOUT 1 CUP)

LEMON SLICES FOR GARNISH

1. Shuck the oysters over a bowl and reserve 1 cup of their liquor. Strain the liquor through dampened cheesecloth into a small bowl. Set both the oysters and liquor aside.

2. In a medium skillet, melt 1 tablespoon of the butter over medium-high heat and sauté the scallions until just softened, about 3 minutes. Remove the scallions and set aside. In the same skillet, melt the remaining tablespoon of butter over medium-high heat and sauté the mushrooms until softened and browned, about 5 minutes. Set aside

3. In a small saucepan, cook the carrots in boiling, salted water to cover over medium-high heat until just barely tender, about 2 minutes. Drain, pat them dry, and set aside. *continued*

4. In a large nonreactive saucepan or soup pot, bring the wine to a boil over medium-high heat. Remove the pan from the heat and let cool a bit. Slowly add the milk and half-and-half, stirring the mixture constantly to prevent curdling. Return the pan to the stove top and, over medium-high heat, bring to a slow boil. Cook, uncovered, until slightly thickened, about 5 minutes. Reduce the heat to medium-low and stir in the reserved oyster liquor. Add the reserved scallions and carrots and cook until heated through, about 5 minutes. Season to taste with salt and pepper.

5. Add the watercress and reserved mushrooms and cook gently for about 2 minutes longer, until heated through, about 2 minutes. Add the reserved oysters and cook, stirring briskly, until their edges just begin to curl, about 1 minute.

6. Ladle the soup into bowls and garnish with the lemon slices. Serve immediately.

cool clam chowder

New England clam chowder is a mainstay of every cook's seafood repertoire. This version, which is blended and served cold, is very smooth and creamy. It's just the thing to bring to the beach in a chilled thermos for a picnic lunch.

SERVES 6

1 DOZEN CHERRYSTONE CLAMS, SCRUBBED AND RINSED	3 MEDIUM RUSSET POTATOES, PEELED AND DICED
2 SLICES BACON	DASH OF HOT SAUCE
2 TABLESPOONS UNSALTED BUTTER	1 CUP WHOLE MILK
1 MEDIUM ONION, FINELY DICED	1 CUP HALF-AND-HALF
1 CUP BOTTLED CLAM JUICE	KOSHER SALT AND FRESHLY GROUND BLACK PEPPER
1 CUP DRY WHITE WINE	2 TABLESPOONS DRY SHERRY
1 TEASPOON CHOPPED FRESH THYME, OR ½ TEASPOON DRIED	½ CUP CHOPPED FRESH FLAT-LEAF PARSLEY FOR GARNISH
1 BAY LEAF	

1. Put the clams in a large pot, add 1 cup of water, cover, and cook over high heat until the clams open, about 10 minutes. Remove the clams from the heat with tongs as they open and put in a colander to cool. (Discard any that do not open.) Strain and reserve the clam broth (you should have about 1 cup). When the clams are cool enough to handle, remove them from their shells, coarsely chop, and reserve.

2. Put the bacon in a large soup pot and fry until crisp. Save the bacon for another use, and pour out and discard all but 1 tablespoon of the bacon fat.

3. Add the butter to the pot and melt over low heat. Add the onion and cook, stirring occasionally, until softened, about 10 minutes. Add 1 cup of water, the clam juice, wine, thyme, bay leaf, and potatoes and bring to a boil. Reduce the heat and simmer until the potatoes are just tender, 20 to 25 minutes.

4. Add the clams and their juice and the hot sauce and simmer for 5 minutes. Stir in the milk, half-and-half, and salt and pepper to taste. Raise the heat to medium, and when the soup is just barely boiling, stir in the sherry. Remove the pot from the heat and let the soup cool for about 1 hour.

5. Purée the soup, in batches, in a blender or food processor. Return the soup to the pot and taste and adjust the seasonings, if necessary. Cover and refrigerate for at least 4 hours before serving, garnished with the parsley.

shellfish chowder

Here is a fantastic dish—a saffron-scented, tomato-based chowder chock-full of clams, mussels, and shrimp. Serve it with grilled baguettes and a bottle of chilled Muscadet for a very impressive main course.

SERVES 6

3 TABLESPOONS OLIVE OIL

I MEDIUM ONION, THINLY SLICED

3 CLOVES GARLIC, THINLY SLICED

I CUP DRY WHITE WINE

I CAN (28 OUNCES) PLUM TOMATOES,
    COARSELY CHOPPED, JUICE RESERVED

6 SPRIGS FRESH FLAT-LEAF PARSLEY,
    PLUS 1/2 CUP CHOPPED

1/4 TEASPOON DRIED THYME

1/4 TEASPOON FENNEL SEED

2 PINCHES OF SAFFRON

I DOZEN LITTLENECK CLAMS,
    SCRUBBED AND RINSED

2 POUNDS MUSSELS, SCRUBBED, DEBEARDED,
    AND RINSED

I POUND LARGE SHRIMP (ABOUT 32 TO 36)

1. Heat the olive oil in a large soup pot over medium-high heat. Cook the onion and garlic until softened, about 5 minutes. Add I cup of water, the wine, and the tomatoes and their juice, raise the heat to high, and cook until just boiling. Reduce the heat to low and add the parsley sprigs, thyme, fennel seed, and saffron. Cook, uncovered, at a gentle simmer for 30 minutes, stirring occasionally. (The chowder base can be made up to this point. Set aside until cool, then refrigerate, covered, for up to 3 days.)

2. Bring the chowder base to a rapid boil. Add the clams, mussels, and shrimp and return to a boil. Cover and cook until the clams and mussels open and the shrimp turn pink, 8 to 10 minutes. (Discard any clams or mussels that do not open.)

3. Ladle the chowder into large soup bowls, garnish with chopped parsley, and serve at once.

red clam chowder

Loaded with cherrystone clams, Yukon Gold potatoes, and fresh herbs, this chowder is a very tasty meal in a bowl.

SERVES 4 TO 6

1 CUP DRY WHITE WINE

6 CLOVES GARLIC, THINLY SLICED

KOSHER SALT AND FRESHLY GROUND
    BLACK PEPPER

1 DOZEN CHERRYSTONE CLAMS,
    SCRUBBED AND RINSED

2 STRIPS BACON

1 TABLESPOON OLIVE OIL

1 MEDIUM ONION, FINELY DICED

2 MEDIUM CARROTS, PEELED AND DICED

2 CELERY RIBS, FINELY DICED

2 TABLESPOONS TOMATO PASTE

1 CAN (28 OUNCES) PLUM TOMATOES,
    COARSELY CHOPPED, JUICE RESERVED

1 TEASPOON CHOPPED FRESH THYME,
    OR $\frac{1}{2}$ TEASPOON DRIED

2 CUPS CHICKEN BROTH, PREFERABLY
    HOMEMADE

2 MEDIUM YUKON GOLD POTATOES,
    PEELED AND CUT INTO $\frac{1}{2}$-INCH CUBES

$\frac{1}{2}$ CUP CHOPPED FRESH FLAT-LEAF PARSLEY

1. Pour the wine into a large pot and add half of the garlic and salt and pepper to taste. Add the clams to the pot, cover, and cook over high heat until open, about 10 minutes. Remove the clams from the pot with tongs as they open and put in a colander to cool. (Discard any that do not open.) Strain and reserve the clam broth (you should have about 1 cup). When the clams are cool enough to handle, remove them from their shells, coarsely chop, and reserve.

2. Put the bacon in a large soup pot and fry until crisp. Drain on paper towels, crumble, and set aside.

3. Add the olive oil, onion, remaining garlic, carrots, and celery to the bacon fat and stir well. Cook, covered, over low heat until softened, about 10 minutes. Add the tomato paste and stir to coat the vegetables. Cook 3 more minutes.

4. Add the tomatoes and their juice and the thyme and cook for another 3 minutes. Add the chicken broth, 1 cup of the reserved clam broth, and 1 cup of water, raise the heat, and bring to a boil. Reduce the heat, add the potatoes, and simmer until the potatoes are tender, about 15 minutes.
5. Add the reserved clams, crumbled bacon, and parsley and cook over low heat until heated through, about 10 minutes. Taste and adjust the seasonings, if necessary, and serve.

lobster & corn chowder

This sublime, creamy chowder is one of my favorite recipes.

SERVES 6

1 OR 2 LOBSTERS (2½ POUNDS TOTAL) BOILED, DRAINED, AND COOLED	3 CUPS CHICKEN BROTH, PREFERABLY HOMEMADE
2 EARS FRESH CORN, HUSKED	1 CUP WHOLE MILK
2 TABLESPOONS UNSALTED BUTTER	½ CUP HEAVY (WHIPPING) CREAM
1 LARGE OR 2 SMALL LEEKS, TRIMMED, RINSED, DRIED, AND CHOPPED	FRESHLY GROUND BLACK PEPPER
1 MEDIUM RED BELL PEPPER, STEMMED, SEEDED, AND FINELY CHOPPED	2 TABLESPOONS CHOPPED FRESH FLAT-LEAF PARSLEY FOR GARNISH
2 TABLESPOONS UNBLEACHED WHITE FLOUR	1 TABLESPOON CHOPPED FRESH CHIVES FOR GARNISH

1. Remove the lobster meat from the shells, pick over, cut into chunks, and set aside.
2. Scrape the kernels from the corn cobs with a small, sharp knife. Reserve with their juices.
3. Melt the butter in a large soup pot over medium-high heat. Sauté the leek for 3 minutes. Add the bell pepper to the pot and sauté for another 3 minutes. Add the flour, stir well, and add the chicken broth. Lower the heat to medium, add the milk and cream, and stir until the soup simmers and thickens slightly. Add the lobster, corn, and pepper to taste and simmer for another 3 minutes, stirring often. Garnish each serving with the herbs and serve at once.

chicken salad niçoise sandwiches

These Mediterranean-inspired sandwiches are perfect to take to the beach for lunch. Wrap them up, pack them in your cooler, and you're good to go.

SERVES 6

1 MEDIUM ONION

2 MEDIUM CARROTS, PEELED

2 CELERY RIBS

6 SPRIGS FRESH FLAT-LEAF PARSLEY,
    PLUS ¼ CUP CHOPPED

3 SPRIGS FRESH THYME, OR
    1 TEASPOON DRIED

1 BAY LEAF

6 WHOLE CLOVES

KOSHER SALT AND FRESHLY GROUND
    BLACK PEPPER

2 WHOLE CHICKEN BREASTS (ABOUT 3
    POUNDS), RINSED AND PATTED DRY

¼ CUP CHOPPED FRESH BASIL

¼ CUP NIÇOISE OLIVES, DRAINED,
    PITTED, AND CHOPPED

2 TABLESPOONS CAPERS, DRAINED

½ CUP CHERRY OR GRAPE TOMATOES,
    HALVED OR QUARTERED

2 TEASPOONS BALSAMIC VINEGAR

1 TEASPOON FRESH LEMON JUICE

⅓ CUP EXTRA-VIRGIN OLIVE OIL

2 LONG BAGUETTES, OR SIX 8-INCH SANDWICH
    ROLLS, HALVED LENGTHWISE

1. Fill a large soup pot with water. Add the onion, carrots, celery, parsley sprigs, thyme, bay leaf, cloves, and salt and pepper to taste. Bring to a boil, reduce the heat, and simmer, uncovered, for 10 minutes.

2. Add the chicken breasts and return to a boil. Reduce the heat, and simmer, partially covered, until the chicken is done, about 20 minutes. Remove the pot from the heat and let the chicken cool in the broth.

3. Remove the chicken from the cooking broth. Reserve the broth for another use. Discard the skin and pull the meat from the bones. Tear into bite-sized pieces and put in a large bowl. Add the chopped parsley, basil, olives, capers, and tomatoes and toss well.

4. Whisk the vinegar, lemon juice, and olive oil together in a small bowl and pour over the chicken mixture. Toss well. Taste and adjust the seasonings, if necessary, and toss again.

5. To assemble the sandwiches, using your hands, hollow out the top and bottom bread halves to create a shell. Discard the insides. Fill the top and bottom halves with the chicken salad, place them together, and press down lightly on them. If using baguettes, cut into thirds crosswise. If using rolls, cut in half crosswise.

lobster rolls

I'm obsessed with lobster rolls and am always searching for the perfect one. I've found that some places are too stingy with the lobster meat and go too easy on the mayonnaise while others go crazy with the mayo. I think I hit it just right while testing lobster rolls this past summer—nothing but fresh lobster, a little chopped celery, and parsley mixed with lemon and paprika-laced mayo, tucked into a toasted hot dog roll. Heaven.

SERVES 6

3 CUPS COOKED LOBSTER MEAT,
   PICKED OVER (SEE NOTE)

3 CELERY RIBS, DICED

¼ CUP CHOPPED FRESH FLAT-LEAF PARSLEY

¾ CUP MAYONNAISE

I TEASPOON DIJON MUSTARD

I TABLESPOON FRESH LEMON JUICE

½ TEASPOON PAPRIKA

KOSHER SALT AND FRESHLY GROUND
   BLACK PEPPER

6 SIDE-SLICED HOT DOG ROLLS

2 TABLESPOONS UNSALTED BUTTER,
   AT ROOM TEMPERATURE (OPTIONAL)

1. Preheat the oven to 350°F.
2. Put the lobster meat, celery, and parsley in a large bowl.
3. Combine the mayonnaise, mustard, lemon juice, paprika, and salt and pepper to taste in a small bowl and mix well. Fold into the lobster and mix well again.
4. Toast the hot dog rolls in the oven or toaster oven until golden brown, being careful not to burn them. Spread them with butter, if desired. Spoon some of the lobster salad into each roll and serve at once.

Note: A 1¼-pound cooked lobster yields about 1 cup of lobster meat.

shrimp burgers with chili mayonnaise

These crispy-fried "burgers" made with fresh shrimp are irresistible. Similar to crab cakes, they're assembled and chilled ahead of time, then fried just until golden.

SERVES 6

2 POUNDS MEDIUM SHRIMP, PEELED,
    DEVEINED, AND CHOPPED
¼ CUP MAYONNAISE
1½ MEDIUM RED ONIONS, 1 MINCED,
    ½ CUT INTO THIN RINGS
1 TEASPOON WORCESTERSHIRE SAUCE
PINCH OF CAYENNE PEPPER
KOSHER SALT AND FRESHLY GROUND
    BLACK PEPPER
1 CUP PLAIN DRY BREAD CRUMBS

SAFFLOWER OIL FOR FRYING

CHILI MAYONNAISE:
½ CUP MAYONNAISE
¼ CUP HOMEMADE OR COMMERCIAL
    CHILI SAUCE

6 HAMBURGER BUNS
2 MEDIUM TOMATOES, SLICED
1 CUP MIXED GREENS

1. Put the shrimp, mayonnaise, minced onion, Worcestershire sauce, cayenne pepper, and salt and pepper to taste in a large bowl and mix well. Shape into 6 wide, flat patties and place on a baking sheet. Cover with plastic wrap and chill in the refrigerator for 4 to 5 hours.

2. Put the bread crumbs on a plate and carefully dredge the patties.

3. Pour the oil in a skillet to a depth of about 1 inch and heat over medium heat until hot, but not smoking. Fry the patties, 3 at a time, until crisp and golden, about 5 minutes per side. Drain on paper towels.

4. To make the Chili Mayonnaise, combine the mayonnaise and chili sauce together in a small bowl and mix well.

5. To assemble the burgers, place the burgers on the buns, and top with tomato slices, onion rings, and lettuce. Spread the underside of the top of each bun with Chili Mayonnaise and serve at once.

fried oyster rolls with spicy tartar sauce

Deliciously decadent fried oysters and spicy tartar sauce are a real treat for a summer lunch.

SERVES 4

¼ CUP UNBLEACHED WHITE FLOUR

I CUP YELLOW CORNMEAL

¼ TEASPOON CAYENNE PEPPER

¼ TEASPOON PAPRIKA

KOSHER SALT AND FRESHLY GROUND
   BLACK PEPPER

2 DOZEN LARGE SHUCKED OYSTERS, DRAINED
   (ABOUT 2 PINTS)

SAFFLOWER OIL FOR FRYING

4 HOT DOG ROLLS, SPLIT AND TOASTED

SPICY TARTAR SAUCE (RECIPE FOLLOWS)

1. Put the flour in a small bowl. In a larger bowl, combine the cornmeal, cayenne pepper, paprika, and salt and pepper to taste and blend well.
2. Dredge the oysters in the flour, then in the cornmeal mixture, shaking off any excess.
3. Pour the oil in a skillet to a depth of about I inch and heat over medium heat until hot, but not smoking. Drop the oysters, a few at a time, in the hot oil and cook, stirring often with a slotted spoon, until golden brown all over, about 2 minutes. Do not overcook. Remove and drain on paper towels. Serve the oysters on toasted hot dog rolls with Spicy Tartar Sauce.

spicy tartar sauce

MAKES ABOUT I ¼ CUPS

I CUP MAYONNAISE

2 TABLESPOONS CHOPPED FRESH CILANTRO

¼ CUP SWEET PICKLE RELISH

8 DASHES OF HOT SAUCE

2 TABLESPOONS FRESH LIME JUICE

I TABLESPOON CHILI POWDER

I TABLESPOON GROUND CUMIN

KOSHER SALT AND FRESHLY GROUND
   BLACK PEPPER

In a medium bowl, stir together the mayonnaise, cilantro, relish, hot sauce, lime juice, chili powder, cumin, and salt and pepper to taste. The sauce will keep, covered, in the refrigerator for up to 3 days.

main courses

boiled lobster with drawn lemon-caper butter • cornmeal-crusted soft-shell crabs with red pepper tartar sauce • clam fritters with tomato-caper sauce • steamed mussels in tomato-fennel broth • garlic shrimp with parsley & basil sauce • linguine with spicy red clam sauce • spaghetti with vongole clam sauce • fried flounder with herbed tartar sauce • red snapper with creamy tomato-basil sauce • baked trout with fennel-walnut stuffing • grilled swordfish with mango salsa • grilled tuna with pineapple relish • cedar-planked salmon in lemon-soy marinade • thai barbecued chicken • citrus-grilled cornish game hens • beach house burgers • country-style ribs with bourbon barbecue sauce • grilled herbed sirloin steak • grilled lamb chops with mint pesto sauce

one of the joys of cooking at the beach is the availability of fresh seafood, whether you're steaming lobsters for a crowd or preparing fish fillets for an elegant dinner party. Be sure to find a good local fish market and ask the fishmonger what is best and freshest. Follow his or her advice to the letter—you won't be sorry you did. Grilling seafood or meat is also an essential part of summertime eating. It's easy, fun, and it's done outdoors. When you're firing up the grill to make Beach House Burgers or Cedar-Planked Salmon, the hot coals and salty air make it all taste better.

boiled lobster with drawn lemon-caper butter

There is nothing more fun or delicious to eat than freshly steamed lobster dipped in butter and lemon. I like to eat lobster outdoors on the deck with baked potatoes and corn on the cob. What a glorious feast!

SERVES 4

3 TABLESPOONS KOSHER SALT

4 LIVE LOBSTERS (1 1/4 TO 1 1/2 POUNDS EACH)

LEMON WEDGES FOR SERVING

LEMON-CAPER BUTTER:

1/2 CUP (1 STICK) UNSALTED BUTTER

1 TEASPOON FRESH LEMON JUICE

1 TEASPOON CAPERS, DRAINED

1 TEASPOON CHOPPED FRESH CHIVES

1. Fill a large soup pot or lobster pot two-thirds full of water. Add the salt and bring to a boil.

2. When the water has come to a rolling boil, plunge the lobsters headfirst into the pot. Cover tightly with the lid and return the water to a boil over high heat. Cook the lobsters until the shells turn bright red, 10 to 12 minutes (see Note).

3. Lift the lobsters out of the water with tongs and drain well in a colander. Remove the rubber bands from the claws, crack the claw shells, and drain off the excess liquid.

4. To make the Lemon-Caper Butter, melt the butter in a small saucepan. Stir in the lemon juice, capers, and chives and keep warm, over very low heat, stirring occasionally, until ready to serve.

5. Serve the lobsters with the butter and lemon wedges.

Note: A rule of thumb for boiling lobsters is
1 1/4- to 1 1/2-pound lobsters, cook 10 to 12 minutes
1 3/4- to 2-pound lobsters, cook 15 to 18 minutes
2 1/2- to 5-pound lobsters, cook 20 to 25 minutes

cornmeal-crusted soft-shell crabs with red pepper tartar sauce

Soft-shell crabs, which appear in late spring and early summer, are scrumptious, especially with a chunky tartar sauce filled with red bell peppers and onions. When buying soft-shells, look for lively ones and ask your fishmonger to clean them. They should be refrigerated immediately and prepared on the same day you buy them.

SERVES 4

2 CUPS WHOLE MILK OR BUTTERMILK

2 LARGE EGGS

8 MEDIUM SOFT-SHELL CRABS, CLEANED

I CUP SELF-RISING CAKE FLOUR,
    SUCH AS PRESTO

I CUP YELLOW CORNMEAL

KOSHER SALT AND FRESHLY GROUND
    BLACK PEPPER

SAFFLOWER OIL FOR FRYING

RED PEPPER TARTAR SAUCE (FACING PAGE)
    FOR SERVING

HOT SAUCE FOR SERVING

LEMON WEDGES FOR SERVING

1. Whisk the buttermilk and eggs together and pour into a large, shallow dish. Add the crabs and soak, covered, in the refrigerator for I to 2 hours.

2. Whisk together the flour, cornmeal, and salt and pepper to taste and transfer to a large plastic bag. Lift a crab out of the buttermilk, letting the excess liquid drip off, and shake in the bag to coat with the flour and cornmeal mixture. Shake off the excess flour and transfer to a plate. Repeat with the remaining crabs and arrange in I layer.

3. Heat the oil in a large skillet to a depth of about $\frac{1}{2}$ inch. Put the crabs in, shell side down, 2 or 3 at a time, and fry until golden brown, turning them over halfway through the frying, 3 to 5 minutes per side. Watch out for popping. Repeat with the remaining crabs, adding more oil if necessary. Drain the crabs on paper towels. Serve with the tartar sauce, hot sauce, and lemon wedges.

red pepper tartar sauce

MAKES ABOUT 1 3/4 CUPS

1 1/2 CUPS MAYONNAISE

2 TABLESPOONS CHOPPED RED BELL PEPPER

2 TABLESPOONS CHOPPED RED ONION

1 TABLESPOON CHOPPED SWEET
    GHERKIN PICKLE

1 TABLESPOON CHOPPED FRESH THYME

2 TABLESPOONS FRESH LEMON JUICE

KOSHER SALT AND FRESHLY GROUND
    BLACK PEPPER

In a medium bowl, stir together the mayonnaise, bell pepper, onion, pickle, thyme, lemon juice, and salt and pepper to taste. The sauce will keep, covered, in the refrigerator for up to 3 days.

clam fritters with tomato-caper sauce

This is an excellent recipe for a basic seafood fritter made with clams, oysters, or shrimp. Here I use chopped chowder clams in their juice, purchased from the fish market. The fritters are delicious served with warm Tomato-Caper Sauce or with Herbed Tartar Sauce and a squeeze of fresh lemon.

SERVES 6

CLAM FRITTERS:

¼ CUP CLAM JUICE

½ CUP WHOLE MILK

2 LARGE EGGS

¾ CUP UNBLEACHED WHITE FLOUR

I TEASPOON BAKING POWDER

⅔ CUP MATZOH OR SALTINE CRACKER
    CRUMBS

2 CUPS CHOPPED FRESH CHOWDER CLAMS,
    DRAINED (ABOUT 2 PINTS)

2 TABLESPOONS CHOPPED FRESH FLAT-LEAF
    PARSLEY

PINCH OF CAYENNE PEPPER

KOSHER SALT AND FRESHLY GROUND
    BLACK PEPPER

TOMATO-CAPER SAUCE:

2 TABLESPOONS OLIVE OIL

½ CUP MINCED SHALLOTS

I CUP FINELY CHOPPED FRESH OR CANNED
    PLUM TOMATOES, WITH THEIR JUICE

I TABLESPOON CAPERS, DRAINED

I TABLESPOON CHOPPED FRESH FLAT-LEAF
    PARSLEY

CANOLA OR SAFFLOWER OIL FOR FRYING

HERBED TARTAR SAUCE (PAGE 73)
    FOR SERVING

LEMON WEDGES FOR SERVING

1. To begin the clam fritters, combine the clam juice, milk, and eggs in a large bowl and whisk thoroughly to combine. Add the flour and baking powder and beat until smooth. Add the matzoh or cracker crumbs and mix well.

2. Stir in the clams, parsley, cayenne pepper, and salt and pepper to taste. Allow the mixture to rest and thicken for at least 20 minutes before frying.

3. Meanwhile, prepare the Tomato-Caper Sauce. Heat the olive oil in a medium sauté pan and cook the shallots over medium heat until softened and golden, about 3 minutes. Add the tomatoes and their juice and bring to a boil. Reduce the heat and simmer for 15 minutes, stirring occasionally. Add the capers and parsley and simmer for an additional 5 minutes. Cover and keep warm until serving.

4. To cook the fritters, pour the oil into a large skillet to a depth of $\frac{1}{2}$ inch. When the oil is very hot, drop the batter by tablespoonfuls into the oil and fry until light golden brown, about 3 minutes. Gently turn them to brown on the other side, about 3 minutes more. Drain on paper towels.

5. Serve the fritters with Tomato-Caper Sauce or Herbed Tartar Sauce and lemon wedges.

steamed mussels
in tomato-fennel broth

Fresh, briny mussels steamed in saffron-scented broth make a light and delicious lunch or dinner. I often prepare the broth ahead of time and always have some on hand in the freezer. Serve this tasty dish with lots of crusty bread, salad, and a crisp white wine.

SERVES 6

2 TABLESPOONS OLIVE OIL

1 MEDIUM WHITE ONION, FINELY CHOPPED

2 SHALLOTS, MINCED

1/2 MEDIUM FENNEL BULB, TRIMMED
   AND THINLY SLICED

1 CUP DRY WHITE WINE

1 CAN (28 OUNCES) PLUM TOMATOES,
   COARSELY CHOPPED, JUICE RESERVED

2 SAFFRON THREADS

FRESHLY GROUND BLACK PEPPER

3 POUNDS MUSSELS, SCRUBBED, DEBEARDED,
   AND RINSED

1/2 CUP CHOPPED FRESH FLAT-LEAF PARSLEY

1. Heat the olive oil in a large soup pot over medium heat. Add the onion, shallots, and fennel and sauté until softened, 10 to 15 minutes.

2. Add the wine and the tomatoes and their juice, bring to a boil, then lower the heat and simmer, partially covered, for 15 minutes. Add the saffron and pepper to taste and simmer an additional 10 minutes. (The broth can be prepared up to this point and refrigerated for up to 1 week, or frozen for up to 1 month).

3. Return the broth to a boil over high heat. Add the mussels and parsley, cover, reduce the heat to medium, and let the mussels steam until they open, about 5 minutes. (Discard any that do not open.)

4. Spoon the mussels and broth into large soup bowls and serve at once.

garlic shrimp with parsley & basil sauce

This is an easy and interesting dish to make, perhaps for weekend guests arriving on Friday night. Make the Parsley and Basil Sauce well ahead of time and assemble all of the ingredients for the Garlic Shrimp. The dish takes about 5 minutes to cook. Your guests will think you're brilliant.

SERVES 4 TO 6

PARSLEY & BASIL SAUCE:

3 TABLESPOONS OLIVE OIL

3 LARGE CLOVES GARLIC, THINLY SLICED

1 CUP COARSELY CHOPPED FRESH BASIL

½ CUP CHOPPED FRESH FLAT-LEAF PARSLEY

4 SCALLIONS, TRIMMED AND MINCED

1 TEASPOON FRESH LEMON JUICE

½ CUP EXTRA-VIRGIN OLIVE OIL

KOSHER SALT AND FRESHLY GROUND
   BLACK PEPPER

GARLIC SHRIMP:

3 TABLESPOONS OLIVE OIL

2 LARGE CLOVES GARLIC, THINLY SLICED

2 POUNDS LARGE SHRIMP (ABOUT 32 TO 36
   PER POUND), PEELED AND DEVEINED

KOSHER SALT AND FRESHLY GROUND
   BLACK PEPPER

½ TEASPOON PAPRIKA

1 TEASPOON FRESH LEMON JUICE

1. To make the Parsley & Basil Sauce, heat the olive oil in a small sauté pan, add the garlic, and cook until softened, 5 to 6 minutes. Transfer the garlic and oil to a food processor. Add the basil, parsley, scallions, and lemon juice and process until well combined. Leave the motor running and add the extra-virgin olive oil in a slow, steady stream. Add the salt and pepper to taste and process again. Taste and adjust the seasonings, if necessary. The sauce will keep, covered, in the refrigerator for up to 3 days. Bring to room temperature and stir well before serving.

2. To make the Garlic Shrimp, heat the olive oil in a large sauté pan over medium heat. Add the garlic and cook until sizzling, about 1 minute. Add the shrimp to the pan and sprinkle with salt and pepper to taste and the paprika. Sauté the shrimp, tossing constantly, until they turn pink, about 3 minutes. Add the lemon juice, toss, and cook an additional 30 seconds.

3. Remove the shrimp from the pan with a slotted spoon, transfer to a platter, and drizzle with the Parsley and Basil Sauce. Serve at once.

linguine with spicy red clam sauce

I love this spicy, gutsy version of red clam sauce. Although it's terrific with linguine, it also works very well with other pastas, such as penne, fusilli, or farfalle.

SERVES 6 AS A FIRST COURSE; 4 AS A MAIN COURSE

I DOZEN CHERRYSTONE CLAMS,
    SCRUBBED AND RINSED

4 CLOVES GARLIC, THINLY SLICED

I CUP DRY WHITE WINE

KOSHER SALT AND FRESHLY GROUND
    BLACK PEPPER

2 TABLESPOONS OLIVE OIL

I LARGE ONION, FINELY CHOPPED

I CAN (28 OUNCES) PLUM TOMATOES,
    COARSELY CHOPPED, JUICE RESERVED

PINCH OF SUGAR

PINCH OF RED PEPPER FLAKES

1/2 CUP CHOPPED FRESH BASIL

1/2 CUP CHOPPED FRESH FLAT-LEAF PARSLEY

I POUND LINGUINE

1. Combine the clams, half the garlic, the wine, and salt and pepper to taste in a large soup pot. Cover and cook over high heat until the clams open, 8 to 10 minutes. (Discard any that do not open.) Transfer the clams to a bowl with tongs or a slotted spoon. Strain and reserve the cooking liquid. (You should have about 1 cup.) When the clams are cool enough to handle, remove them from their shells, chop coarsely, and reserve.

2. Heat the olive oil in a large sauté pan and cook the onion and remaining garlic over medium heat until softened and golden, about 5 minutes. Add the tomatoes and their juice, sugar, and salt and pepper to taste and simmer, uncovered, over very low heat for about 30 minutes, stirring occasionally.

3. About 10 minutes before serving, stir in 1/2 cup of the reserved clam juice, the clams, red pepper flakes, basil, and parsley and simmer the sauce for about 10 more minutes, stirring occasionally. Add a bit more clam juice to the sauce if it seems too thick.

4. Meanwhile, bring a large pot of salted water to a boil and cook the linguine until al dente. Drain immediately. Divide the pasta into large soup or pasta bowls, top each serving with the sauce, and serve at once.

spaghetti with vongole clam sauce

Spaghetti and clam sauce is a great dish for weekend cooking. It can be made on a moment's notice, as long as you have the clams, and it tastes fantastic. I like to make it with vongole clams, which are very tiny and sweet-tasting. The sauce is also excellent with Manila or littleneck clams. When making spaghetti and clam sauce, be sure to toss the pasta with the sauce in the pot before serving so the sauce adheres to each strand of spaghetti.

SERVES 6 AS A FIRST COURSE; 4 AS A MAIN COURSE

3 STRIPS BACON

1 POUND SPAGHETTI

2 TABLESPOONS OLIVE OIL

1 SMALL ONION, FINELY CHOPPED

2 CLOVES GARLIC, THINLY SLICED

1 1/2 TO 2 POUNDS VONGOLE, MANILA, OR LITTLENECK CLAMS, SCRUBBED AND RINSED

1 CUP DRY WHITE WINE

PINCH OF RED PEPPER FLAKES

1/2 CUP CHOPPED FRESH FLAT-LEAF PARSLEY

FRESHLY GROUND BLACK PEPPER

1. Cook the bacon over medium heat in a large skillet or sauté pan with a lid until crisp. Remove the bacon and drain on paper towels, leaving the drippings in the pan. When cool enough to handle, crumble the bacon.

2. Bring a large pot of salted water to a boil and cook the spaghetti until al dente.

3. Meanwhile, add the olive oil to the bacon drippings and heat. Add the onion and garlic and cook over medium heat until softened and golden, about 7 minutes. Add the clams, wine, and red pepper flakes. Raise the heat to high and cover and cook until all the clams are open, 3 to 5 minutes. (Discard any that do not open.)

4. Drain the pasta and return to the pot. Add the clam sauce, parsley, and reserved bacon to the pasta and toss well. Season with pepper to taste and serve at once.

fried flounder
with herbed tartar sauce

Lemony fried fish fillets served with a homemade tartar sauce packed with fresh herbs from the garden make a simple and delicious meal. I prefer flounder, but any mild, white-fleshed fish, such as bass or snapper, will be very tasty.

SERVES 6

¾ CUP UNBLEACHED WHITE FLOUR,
    PLUS MORE FOR COATING

¼ TEASPOON BAKING SODA

KOSHER SALT AND FRESHLY GROUND
    BLACK PEPPER

I CUP WHOLE MILK

I LARGE EGG, LIGHTLY BEATEN

2 TABLESPOONS CLUB SODA

2 TEASPOONS FRESH LEMON JUICE

CANOLA OR SAFFLOWER OIL FOR FRYING

12 FLOUNDER FILLETS (ABOUT 6 OUNCES
    EACH), RINSED AND PATTED DRY

HERBED TARTAR SAUCE (FACING PAGE)

1. In a large, shallow bowl, whisk together the ¾ cup flour, baking soda, and salt and pepper to taste. Stir in the milk, egg, club soda, and lemon juice and set aside for 30 minutes.

2. Spread about ½ inch of flour in a shallow dish.

3. Heat about 1 inch of oil in a large skillet or 2 medium skillets over high heat.

4. Lay each fillet in the flour and turn to coat, shaking off the excess flour. Dip the fillet in the batter and then let the excess drip back into the bowl. Fry the fillets, in batches if necessary, turning once with tongs, until golden brown and cooked through, about 6 minutes. Drain on paper towels. If working in batches, cover the fish and keep them warm in a low (200°F) oven. Serve immediately with Herbed Tartar Sauce.

herbed tartar sauce

This tasty tartar sauce, made with homemade mayonnaise, is very easy to make with a food processor. The ingredients, which should be at room temperature, will blend into a silken sauce when you add the oils in a slow, steady stream through the feed tube. If you have any concern regarding the raw egg in the recipe, use commercial mayonnaise instead.

MAKES ABOUT 1 1/4 CUPS

1 LARGE EGG	2 TABLESPOONS CHOPPED DILL PICKLE
1 TABLESPOON FRESH LEMON JUICE	1 TABLESPOON CAPERS, DRAINED
1 TEASPOON DIJON MUSTARD	1 TABLESPOON CHOPPED FRESH CHIVES
PINCH OF SALT	1 TABLESPOON CHOPPED FRESH TARRAGON
DASH OF HOT SAUCE	1 TABLESPOON CHOPPED FRESH
3/4 CUP SAFFLOWER OIL	FLAT-LEAF PARSLEY
1/4 CUP EXTRA-VIRGIN OLIVE OIL	FRESHLY GROUND BLACK PEPPER

1. In the bowl of a food processor, combine the egg, lemon juice, mustard, salt, and hot sauce. With the motor running, slowly pour the oils through the feed tube in a steady stream. When thoroughly blended, turn off the machine, scrape down the sides, and taste and adjust the seasonings, if necessary. Scrape into a container, cover, and refrigerate for up to 5 days.

2. About 1 hour before serving, fold the pickle, capers, chives, tarragon, and parsley into the mayonnaise. Season to taste with pepper. Cover and refrigerate until serving.

red snapper with
creamy tomato-basil sauce

Red snapper is a mild and fairly sweet-tasting fish. It's especially delicious with this light cream sauce, which is prepared with garden-fresh tomatoes and basil. You can also use another type of snapper, or sole, or orange roughy in this dish. For a very special summertime dinner party, serve the fish with lemon-roasted potatoes and mixed greens.

SERVES 6

3 TABLESPOONS OLIVE OIL

6 RED SNAPPER FILLETS
    (ABOUT 8 OUNCES EACH)

KOSHER SALT AND FRESHLY GROUND
    BLACK PEPPER

2 CLOVES GARLIC, THINLY SLICED

1 1/2 CUPS CHOPPED RIPE TOMATO

3 TABLESPOONS CHOPPED FRESH BASIL

3 TO 4 TABLESPOONS HEAVY
    (WHIPPING) CREAM

1. Put 1 1/2 tablespoons of the olive oil in a large nonstick skillet and add the fillets, turning to coat with the oil on both sides. Arrange the fish, skinned sides down, and season with salt and pepper to taste. Cover and cook the fish over low heat until just cooked through, about 10 minutes. Transfer the fillets to a platter, cover with foil, and set aside.

2. Add the remaining 1 1/2 tablespoons of olive oil to the skillet and sauté the garlic until softened, about 2 minutes. Add the tomato and cook for about 1 minute, then add 2 tablespoons of the basil and cook for another minute. Stir in the cream and cook until just warmed through, about 2 minutes.

3. Pour the tomato-cream sauce over the fish and garnish with the remaining tablespoon of basil. Serve at once.

baked trout with fennel-walnut stuffing

Here is a delectable way to prepare trout, which is usually available at fish markets year-round. You can use either brook, lake, or rainbow trout in this recipe. Have your fishmonger clean and fillet the whole fish, leaving the heads and tails on.

SERVES 6

I TABLESPOON UNSALTED BUTTER

I TABLESPOON OLIVE OIL, PLUS MORE
   FOR BRUSHING

I MEDIUM ONION, FINELY CHOPPED

I MEDIUM FENNEL BULB, TRIMMED
   AND FINELY CHOPPED

1/2 CUP CHOPPED WALNUTS

1/2 CUP CHOPPED FRESH FLAT-LEAF PARSLEY

KOSHER SALT AND FRESHLY GROUND
   BLACK PEPPER

6 FRESH TROUT (ABOUT 12 OUNCES EACH),
   CLEANED AND FILLETED, HEADS AND TAILS
   LEFT ON

I MEDIUM LEMON, THINLY SLICED

1. Heat the butter and I tablespoon olive oil over medium heat in a large sauté pan. Add the onion and cook until softened and golden, about 7 minutes. Add the fennel and cook until just tender, about 5 minutes. Add the walnuts, parsley, and salt and pepper to taste and cook an additional 5 minutes, stirring often.

2. Preheat the oven to 350°F.

3. Place the fish on a foil-lined baking sheet brushed with a bit of olive oil. Brush the inside surface of each fish with an additional bit of olive oil. Spoon about 3 tablespoons of the stuffing into the cavity of each fish and spread evenly. Brush the top of each stuffed fish with a bit of olive oil and place 2 or 3 lemon slices over it. Sprinkle the fish with salt to taste and bake in the top third of the oven until the skin is crisp, about 15 minutes. Serve at once.

grilled swordfish with mango salsa

Swordfish is an excellent fish for grilling because its meat is firm and its relatively high oil content keeps it moist. It pairs well with a strongly flavored accompaniment, such as this spicy Mango Salsa. The salsa, which is also terrific with tortilla chips, can be made well ahead of time.

SERVES 6

MANGO SALSA:

2 SMALL TOMATOES, CORED AND DICED

1/2 MEDIUM RED OR YELLOW BELL PEPPER, STEMMED, SEEDED, AND DICED

2 SCALLIONS, TRIMMED AND MINCED

1/2 MEDIUM RED ONION, DICED

I RIPE MANGO, PEELED, PITTED, AND DICED

1/4 CUP CHOPPED FRESH CILANTRO

1/4 CUP CHOPPED FRESH FLAT-LEAF PARSLEY

I TABLESPOON ORANGE JUICE

I TABLESPOON FRESH LIME JUICE

PINCH OF RED PEPPER FLAKES

KOSHER SALT AND FRESHLY GROUND BLACK PEPPER

6 SWORDFISH STEAKS (ABOUT 8 OUNCES EACH), ABOUT I INCH THICK

OLIVE OIL FOR BRUSHING

KOSHER SALT AND FRESHLY GROUND BLACK PEPPER

1. To make the Mango Salsa, combine the tomatoes, bell pepper, scallions, onion, mango, cilantro, parsley, orange juice, lime juice, red pepper flakes, and salt and pepper to taste in a large bowl and mix well. Taste and adjust the seasonings. The salsa will keep, covered, in the refrigerator for up to 3 days.

2. Prepare a gas or charcoal grill. Brush the fish lightly with the olive oil and sprinkle with salt and pepper to taste. When the fire is medium-hot, and the coals are covered with a light coating of ash and glow deep red, grill the fish until it is opaque throughout, 4 to 5 minutes per side.

3. Spoon a generous portion of the salsa over each steak and serve at once.

grilled tuna with pineapple relish

It's hard to go wrong grilling fresh tuna because it cooks like steak and almost never sticks. I like to serve these tuna steaks with tangy pineapple relish.

SERVES 6

PINEAPPLE RELISH:

1 CUP CHOPPED FRESH PINEAPPLE

½ MEDIUM RED BELL PEPPER, STEMMED,
    SEEDED, AND DICED

2 SCALLIONS, TRIMMED AND MINCED

1 TABLESPOON MINCED FRESH GINGER

1 TABLESPOON FRESH LIME JUICE

1 TABLESPOON LOW-SODIUM SOY SAUCE

1 TEASPOON TOASTED SESAME OIL

1 TEASPOON SUGAR

6 TUNA STEAKS (ABOUT 8 OUNCES EACH),
    ABOUT 1½ INCHES THICK

OLIVE OIL FOR BRUSHING

KOSHER SALT AND FRESHLY GROUND
    BLACK PEPPER

1. To make the relish, combine the pineapple, bell pepper, scallions, ginger, lime juice, soy sauce, sesame oil, and sugar in a medium bowl and mix well. Taste and adjust the seasonings, if necessary.

2. Prepare a gas or charcoal grill. Brush the fish lightly with the olive oil and sprinkle with salt and pepper to taste. When the fire is medium-hot, and the coals are covered with a light coating of ash and glow deep red, grill the fish until it is opaque, 4 to 5 minutes per side.

3. Spoon a generous portion of the relish over or beside each steak and serve at once.

cedar-planked salmon in lemon-soy marinade

Salmon cooked on a cedar plank over a hot fire has a fantastic, smoky flavor. Cedar planks have become very popular and are available at fish markets and gourmet shops, and can also be bought online. In this recipe, the fish marinates for a few hours in a lemon-soy mixture before it is cooked on the plank over a hot fire. Be sure to follow manufacturer's instructions for soaking the planks before using.

SERVES 6

LEMON-SOY MARINADE:

1/2 CUP LOW-SODIUM SOY SAUCE OR
    PONZU SAUCE (SEE NOTE)

1/2 CUP ASIAN BARBECUE SAUCE (SEE NOTE)

JUICE OF 1 MEDIUM LEMON

2 TABLESPOONS GRATED FRESH GINGER

1 SALMON FILLET (5 TO 6 POUNDS)

1. To make the marinade, whisk the soy or ponzu sauce, barbecue sauce, lemon juice, and ginger together in a small bowl. Put the salmon in a baking dish and pour the marinade over it. Cover and refrigerate for about 2 hours.

2. Soak a cedar plank in cold water for at least 2 hours, or according to the manufacturer's instructions.

3. Prepare a gas or charcoal grill. When the fire is hot, and the coals are covered with a light coating of ash and glow deep red, put the plank on the grill, using long tongs. Heat the plank until it becomes very hot and smokes and crackles. Carefully place the fish on the plank, cover, and cook until nicely smoked and cooked through, about 15 minutes. Serve at once.

Note: Ponzu sauce and Asian barbecue sauce are available at Asian markets, health food stores, and ethnic sections of supermarkets.

thai barbecued chicken

Chicken marinated in coconut milk, nam pla (Asian fish sauce), lime juice, and other savory ingredients is delicious when cooked on the grill. This recipe also works very well with chicken wings and drumettes for tasty appetizers.

SERVES 6

1 CUP COCONUT MILK	½ CUP CHOPPED FRESH CILANTRO
⅓ CUP NAM PLA (SEE NOTE)	KOSHER SALT AND FRESHLY GROUND
¼ CUP FRESH LIME JUICE	BLACK PEPPER
4 CLOVES GARLIC, MINCED	1 CHICKEN (2½ TO 3 POUNDS), CUT INTO
2 SHALLOTS, MINCED	10 PIECES, OR 8 CHICKEN THIGHS
1 TEASPOON HOT SAUCE	(BONES IN)
1 TEASPOON RED PEPPER FLAKES	6 SCALLIONS, TRIMMED AND MINCED,
1½ TABLESPOONS SUGAR	FOR GARNISH

1. Combine the coconut milk, nam pla, lime juice, garlic, shallots, hot sauce, red pepper flakes, sugar, cilantro, and salt and pepper to taste in a blender and blend until smooth. Put the chicken in a large nonreactive bowl or baking dish. Pour the mixture over the chicken and marinate for 4 hours in the refrigerator, turning the chicken occasionally.

2. Prepare a gas or charcoal grill. When the fire is medium-hot, and the coals are covered with a light coating of ash and glow deep red, put the chicken on the grill, bone side down. Cover and cook for about 15 minutes. Turn and cook, skin side down, covered, until the juices run clear, 12 to 15 minutes.

3. Transfer the chicken to a platter, garnish with the scallions, and serve at once.

Note: Nam pla is available in Asian and Indian markets.

citrus-grilled cornish game hens

Cornish game hens bathed in a marinade of lime and orange juice, garlic, and olive oil are a natural for grilling. They're delicious served hot, cold, or at room temperature and are perfect for a picnic.

SERVES 6

4 CORNISH GAME HENS
(ABOUT 1¼ POUNDS EACH), HALVED

½ CUP FRESH LIME JUICE (ABOUT 4 LIMES)

½ CUP ORANGE JUICE

3 CLOVES GARLIC, THINLY SLICED

2 TABLESPOONS EXTRA-VIRGIN OLIVE OIL

KOSHER SALT AND FRESHLY GROUND
BLACK PEPPER

2 BUNCHES WATERCRESS, STEMMED,
FOR GARNISH

1. Put the hens in a large, shallow glass or ceramic bowl. In another bowl, whisk together the lime juice, orange juice, garlic, olive oil, and salt and pepper to taste. Pour the marinade over the hens and turn to coat them thoroughly. Cover the bowl with plastic wrap and refrigerate the hens for 4 to 6 hours, turning them occasionally.

2. Preheat the oven to 350°F. Prepare a gas or charcoal grill.

3. Transfer the hens and half of the marinade to a shallow baking pan. Reserve the remaining half of the marinade for basting. Bake the hens for 20 minutes and remove them from the oven.

4. When the fire is medium-hot, and the coals are covered with a light coating of ash and glow deep red, grill the hens, basting them often with the marinade, until nicely browned and the juices run clear, about 10 minutes per side.

5. Scatter the watercress to cover a large platter and place the hens over it. Serve at once.

beach house burgers

Sometimes you've just got to have a burger. I love to grill them after a long afternoon at the beach, and one of my favorite ways to serve them is with a slice of melted mozzarella cheese (plain or smoked) and a big spoonful of chopped fresh tomatoes tossed with basil.

SERVES 8

1 POUND GROUND SIRLOIN

1 POUND GROUND CHUCK

1/2 CUP CHOPPED ONION

KOSHER SALT AND FRESHLY GROUND
    BLACK PEPPER

1 1/2 CUPS CHOPPED FRESH TOMATOES
    (ABOUT 2 TOMATOES)

2 TABLESPOONS CHOPPED FRESH BASIL

8 SLICES PLAIN OR SMOKED
    MOZZARELLA CHEESE

8 HAMBURGER BUNS

1. Put the ground sirloin and chuck, onion, and salt and pepper to taste in a large bowl and mix together with your hands. Form into ¾-inch-thick patties.

2. Mix the chopped tomatoes and basil together in a medium bowl until well combined. Set aside.

3. Prepare a gas or charcoal grill. When the fire is medium-hot, and the coals are covered with a light coating of ash and glow deep red, grill the burgers, 3 to 4 minutes per side for medium-rare. In the last minute of grilling, place a slice of cheese over each burger and cook until the cheese is just melted.

4. Serve the burgers on the hamburger buns and top each burger with a large spoonful of the tomato mixture.

country-style ribs with bourbon barbecue sauce

These country-style spare ribs are fabulous to serve to a hungry crowd for a summer barbecue. The pungent Bourbon Barbecue Sauce, which can be made up to 5 days ahead of time, is used as both a basting and dipping sauce for the ribs. The Spicy Dry Rub is applied to the ribs a day ahead of time.

SERVES 6 TO 8

BOURBON BARBECUE SAUCE:

2 SLICES BACON

1 ½ CUPS KETCHUP

¼ CUP MOLASSES

2 TABLESPOONS CIDER VINEGAR

2 TABLESPOONS WORCESTERSHIRE SAUCE

2 TABLESPOONS LOW-SODIUM SOY SAUCE

2 TABLESPOONS BOURBON

2 TABLESPOONS STRONG BLACK COFFEE

1 TEASPOON DIJON MUSTARD

1 TEASPOON ONION POWDER

DASH OF HOT SAUCE

SPICY DRY RUB:

2 TEASPOONS KOSHER SALT

1 TABLESPOON ONION POWDER OR FLAKES

1 TEASPOON GARLIC SALT

2 TEASPOONS DRIED OREGANO

1 TEASPOON DRIED THYME

2 TEASPOONS PAPRIKA

1 TEASPOON CAYENNE PEPPER

1 TEASPOON GROUND CUMIN

2 TEASPOONS DRY MUSTARD

3 RACKS SPARE RIBS (ABOUT 6 POUNDS)

1. To make the Bourbon Barbecue Sauce, cook the bacon until very crisp. Drain, crumble, and set aside. Combine the ketchup, molasses, vinegar, Worcestershire sauce, soy sauce, bourbon, coffee, mustard, onion powder, and hot sauce in a nonreactive saucepan. Bring to a boil, reduce the heat, and simmer over low heat for 30 minutes, stirring occasionally. Stir in the crumbled bacon. The sauce will keep, covered, in the refrigerator for up to 5 days.

2. The day before serving, make the Spicy Dry Rub. Mix together the salt, onion powder, garlic salt, oregano, thyme, paprika, cayenne pepper, cumin, and dry mustard.

3. Sprinkle the spare ribs with water and baste them with the dry rub, using your hands or a brush. Cover and refrigerate for 24 hours.

4. Prepare a gas or charcoal grill. When the fire is medium to medium-low, and the coals are covered with a light coating of ash, grill the ribs, covered, until tender and juicy, about 35 minutes. Baste them often with $1/2$ cup of the Barbecue Sauce. Heat the remaining sauce on the stove and serve warm with the ribs.

grilled herbed sirloin steak

This is a good dish to serve for a casual dinner party. Let the steaks marinate in a fresh herb–infused mixture of olive oil and lemon before cooking them on the grill. They're delicious served with Cherry Tomato, Basil & Feta Cheese Salad (page 104) and fresh corn on the cob.

SERVES 6 TO 8

½ CUP CHOPPED FRESH FLAT-LEAF PARSLEY

¼ CUP CHOPPED FRESH THYME

¼ CUP CHOPPED FRESH ROSEMARY

1 TABLESPOON CHOPPED FRESH SAGE

6 CLOVES GARLIC, HALVED

JUICE OF 1 MEDIUM LEMON

¾ CUP EXTRA-VIRGIN OLIVE OIL

4 TO 5 POUNDS BONELESS SIRLOIN STEAK

KOSHER SALT AND FRESHLY GROUND
    BLACK PEPPER

1. Put the parsley, thyme, rosemary, sage, garlic, and lemon juice in a food processor and pulse until combined. Add the olive oil in a slow, steady stream and process until very smooth.

2. Season the steaks generously with salt and pepper and spread the herb mixture over them on both sides. Cover with foil and refrigerate for 3 to 4 hours.

3. Prepare a gas or charcoal grill. When the fire is medium-hot, and the coals are covered with a light coating of ash and glow deep red, grill the steaks for 5 to 7 minutes per side for medium-rare, or until the desired doneness. Let the steak rest for 10 minutes before slicing. Slice the steak, against the grain, into ¼-inch slices and serve at once.

grilled lamb chops with mint pesto sauce

Tender and flavorful grilled lamb chops taste great with pesto sauce made with garden-fresh basil, parsley, and mint. Orzo, Corn & Chive Salad (page 112) is a very good accompaniment to the chops.

SERVES 6

MINT PESTO SAUCE:

1/2 CUP, PLUS 1 TABLESPOON EXTRA-VIRGIN
    OLIVE OIL

2 CLOVES GARLIC, PEELED

1/4 CUP PINE NUTS

1 CUP FRESH BASIL

1/2 CUP FRESH FLAT-LEAF PARSLEY

1/2 CUP FRESH MINT LEAVES

1 TABLESPOON FRESH LEMON JUICE

KOSHER SALT AND FRESHLY GROUND
    BLACK PEPPER

12 LOIN OR RIB LAMB CHOPS,
    EACH ABOUT 2 INCHES THICK

FRESHLY GROUND BLACK PEPPER

1. To make the Mint Pesto Sauce, heat the 1 tablespoon of the olive oil in a small sauté pan over medium heat and cook the garlic until softened and golden, about 5 minutes. Transfer the garlic to a food processor.

2. Add the pine nuts, basil, parsley, and mint to the food processor and process. Leave the motor running and add the remaining 1/2 cup of olive oil in a slow, steady stream through the feed tube. Process until very smooth. Add the lemon juice and salt and pepper to taste.

3. Season the lamb chops generously with pepper.

4. Prepare a gas or charcoal grill and lightly spray the grill rack with vegetable oil spray. When the fire is medium-hot, and the coals are covered with a light coating of ash and glow deep red, grill the lamb chops for 5 to 6 minutes per side for medium-rare, or until the desired doneness. Season with a bit more pepper before serving, if desired. Serve at once with the pesto sauce on the side.

salads & side dishes

shrimp & snap pea salad with ginger-soy vinaigrette •
lobster & roasted vegetable salad with garlic
vinaigrette • ceviche salad with avocados & tomatoes •
warm scallop & fingerling potato salad • poached
salmon salad with dill vinaigrette • chicken & soba
noodle salad with spicy asian peanut sauce • blt salad
with buttermilk–blue cheese dressing • fennel, orange
& red onion salad • cherry tomato, basil & feta cheese
salad • radicchio, red cabbage & apple slaw • roasted
potato & green bean salad with dijon-horseradish
vinaigrette • grilled sweet potatoes • grilled eggplant &
red peppers • mixed bean salad with chive vinaigrette •
orzo, corn & chive salad • fresh corn fritters

salads are mainstays of warm weather meals, and they are a delight to make when the freshest produce is available from local farmstands and weekend green markets. There are recipes for a variety of salads in this chapter—main course salads starring lobster, shrimp, or salmon; cool starters such as ceviche with scallops; and all kinds of other salads and side dishes made with the season's treasures. When shopping at the farmstand and the fish market, pick ingredients that look sparkling-fresh and then decide what kind of salad to put together and serve. That's what summer cooking is all about.

shrimp & snap pea salad with ginger-soy vinaigrette

Snap peas, sometimes called sugar snap peas, are a cross between the snow pea and the shell pea. They are usually at their peak in late spring and early summer and they pair beautifully with shrimp in this stylish salad, which looks as good as it tastes.

SERVES 4 AS A MAIN COURSE

1½ POUNDS LARGE SHRIMP
   (ABOUT 32 TO 36 PER POUND)

2 CUPS SNAP PEAS (ABOUT ½ POUND),
   TRIMMED

3 SCALLIONS, TRIMMED AND MINCED

GINGER-SOY VINAIGRETTE:

½ CUP EXTRA-VIRGIN OLIVE OIL

2 TABLESPOONS LOW-SODIUM SOY SAUCE

2 TABLESPOONS WHITE VINEGAR

2 TABLESPOONS FRESH LIME JUICE

1 TABLESPOON MINCED FRESH GINGER

3 TO 5 DASHES OF HOT SAUCE

½ CUP DICED MANGO FOR GARNISH

½ CUP CHOPPED PEANUTS OR CASHEWS
   FOR GARNISH

LIME WEDGES FOR GARNISH

1. Bring a large pot of salted water to a boil. Add the shrimp and cook until they turn pink, 3 to 4 minutes. Drain, run under cold water, peel and devein.

2. Meanwhile, bring another pot of salted water to a boil, drop in the snap peas and boil, uncovered, until just tender and still bright green, 2 to 3 minutes. Drain and rinse immediately with cold water to stop the cooking.

3. To make the vinaigrette, whisk together the olive oil, soy sauce, vinegar, lime juice, ginger, and hot sauce in a small bowl until well combined.

4. Put the shrimp, snap peas, and the scallions in a large bowl, add the vinaigrette, and toss well. Divide the mixture among 4 plates and garnish each serving with some of the diced mango, chopped nuts, and lime wedges.

lobster & roasted vegetable salad with garlic vinaigrette

This is a terrific salad to make for a special lunch. Although it may seem a bit labor-intensive, all of the components can be made ahead of time, and the salad can be assembled just before serving.

SERVES 4 AS A MAIN COURSE

GARLIC VINAIGRETTE:

8 CLOVES GARLIC, PEELED

⅓ CUP EXTRA-VIRGIN OLIVE OIL

1 TABLESPOON BALSAMIC VINEGAR

1 TABLESPOON SHERRY VINEGAR

1 TABLESPOON FRESH TARRAGON

KOSHER SALT AND FRESHLY GROUND
    BLACK PEPPER

1½ POUNDS NEW POTATOES,
    CUT INTO 1-INCH CUBES

2 TABLESPOONS OLIVE OIL

1 TABLESPOON KOSHER SALT

1 POUND BEETS, TRIMMED

3 CUPS COOKED LOBSTER MEAT,
    PICKED OVER

1 TABLESPOON FRESH LEMON JUICE

2 BUNCHES ARUGULA, TRIMMED

1. Preheat the oven to 350°F.
2. To make the Garlic Vinaigrette, put the garlic in a small baking dish and cover with the olive oil. Roast the garlic for 10 minutes, turn with a slotted spoon, and roast until golden brown, about 10 minutes. Set aside to cool.
3. Transfer the garlic and 2 tablespoons of the roasting oil to a blender. Add ¼ cup of water, the vinegars, tarragon, and salt and pepper to taste and blend until smooth, adding a bit more water if necessary. The vinaigrette will keep, covered, in the refrigerator, for up to 1 week.

4. To prepare the vegetables, put the potatoes on a baking sheet, add 1 tablespoon of the olive oil and the salt and toss to combine. Wrap the beets in tin foil and place on a separate baking sheet. Roast the potatoes and beets until fork-tender, about 1 hour. Remove from the oven and set aside to cool. Put the potatoes in a medium bowl and toss with 2 tablespoons of the vinaigrette. Remove the beets from the foil, peel, put in a separate medium bowl and toss with 1 tablespoon of the vinaigrette.

5. Put the lobster in a medium bowl, add the remaining tablespoon of olive oil and the lemon juice, and toss lightly.

6. Divide the arugula among 4 plates, and top each serving with some of the potatoes and beets. Spoon the lobster over the vegetables, drizzle with the remaining vinaigrette, and serve.

ceviche salad with avocados & tomatoes

Ceviche is a wonderfully cooling dish and is very easy to prepare. Simply let fresh scallops "cook" in a citrus bath of lemons and limes in the refrigerator.

SERVES 6

1 POUND SEA SCALLOPS, HALVED

1/2 CUP FRESH LIME JUICE (ABOUT 4 LIMES)

2 TABLESPOONS FRESH LEMON JUICE

1/2 MEDIUM RED BELL PEPPER, STEMMED, SEEDED, AND DICED

1/2 MEDIUM YELLOW BELL PEPPER, STEMMED, SEEDED, AND DICED

1 JALAPEÑO PEPPER, SEEDED AND FINELY DICED

3 SCALLIONS, TRIMMED AND MINCED

3 TABLESPOONS CHOPPED FRESH CILANTRO

3 TABLESPOONS EXTRA-VIRGIN OLIVE OIL

KOSHER SALT AND FRESHLY GROUND BLACK PEPPER

2 MEDIUM AVOCADOS, PEELED, PITTED, AND DICED

2 MEDIUM TOMATOES, CORED AND DICED

6 CUPS MIXED SALAD GREENS

LIME WEDGES FOR GARNISH

1. Put the scallops in a large glass bowl and pour over the lemon and lime juices. Add the bell and jalapeño peppers, scallions, and cilantro and toss together. Add 2 tablespoons of the olive oil and salt and pepper to taste and toss thoroughly to coat. Cover and refrigerate, allowing the scallops to "cook" and the flavors to blend, for 2 to 3 hours. Drain the ceviche. Return to the refrigerator if not serving immediately.

2. Put the avocados and tomatoes in a medium bowl with the remaining tablespoon of olive oil and toss gently.

3. Divide the salad greens among 6 plates and top with the avocados and tomatoes. Spoon the ceviche over them and serve, garnished with lime wedges.

warm scallop & fingerling potato salad

I enjoy making all kinds of salads, and I especially like preparing warm salads. They are delicious comfort food and make a surprisingly indulgent starter or main course. This is a wonderful one to make in autumn, when fresh, tender bay scallops become available.

SERVES 6

4 FINGERLING POTATOES, RINSED

1 CUP DRY WHITE WINE

2 SHALLOTS, MINCED

PINCH OF RED PEPPER FLAKES

4 TABLESPOONS OLIVE OIL

1/2 POUND BAY SCALLOPS

1 CUP CHERRY OR GRAPE TOMATOES, HALVED

1/4 CUP WHITE WINE VINEGAR

1 TEASPOON SUGAR

KOSHER SALT AND FRESHLY GROUND
BLACK PEPPER

1 BUNCH WATERCRESS, STEMMED

1. Bring a pot of salted water to a boil. Add the potatoes, reduce the heat, and simmer until fork-tender, about 15 minutes. Drain and return to the pot, covered, to keep warm.

2. Combine the wine, shallots, and red pepper flakes in a small saucepan. Bring to a boil, reduce the heat, and simmer for 2 minutes. Set aside.

3. Heat 2 tablespoons of the olive oil in a nonstick skillet. Add the scallops and sauté for 1 minute. Stir in the tomatoes and continue cooking until they are warmed through, 2 to 3 minutes. Transfer the scallop mixture to a large bowl. Cut the potatoes into 1/2-inch slices and add to the bowl.

4. Return the skillet to the heat, add the wine-shallot mixture and bring to a boil. Add the vinegar and sugar and stir well. Let the mixture boil until reduced to about 1/3 cup. Turn off the heat, whisk in the remaining 2 tablespoons of olive oil, and season with salt and pepper to taste. Pour about half of the vinaigrette over the scallop mixture and toss gently to combine.

5. Arrange the watercress on 6 salad plates. Spoon some of the scallop mixture over each serving and drizzle with a bit more vinaigrette if necessary. Season with additional salt and pepper, if necessary, and serve at once.

poached salmon salad
with dill vinaigrette

There is nothing more simple yet elegant to serve than poached salmon laced with fresh dill vinaigrette. When buying salmon fillets for this salad, be sure to have them skinned.

SERVES 4 AS A MAIN COURSE

POACHED SALMON:

4 SALMON FILLETS (ABOUT 6 OUNCES EACH),
   SKINNED

I CUP DRY WHITE WINE

I SMALL ONION, COARSELY CHOPPED

2 MEDIUM CARROTS, PEELED
   AND COARSELY CHOPPED

6 SPRIGS FRESH FLAT-LEAF PARSLEY

6 WHOLE PEPPERCORNS

4 WHOLE CLOVES

PINCH OF KOSHER SALT

2 CUPS SNAP PEAS ($1/2$ POUND), TRIMMED

DILL VINAIGRETTE:

I TABLESPOON WHITE VINEGAR

I TABLESPOON DIJON MUSTARD

$1/2$ CUP EXTRA-VIRGIN OLIVE OIL

2 TABLESPOONS CHOPPED FRESH DILL

KOSHER SALT AND FRESHLY GROUND
   BLACK PEPPER

2 BUNCHES WATERCRESS, STEMMED

2 TABLESPOONS EXTRA-VIRGIN OLIVE OIL

16 CHERRY TOMATOES, HALVED, FOR GARNISH

16 BLACK OLIVES FOR GARNISH

1. To poach the salmon, put the salmon fillets in a large sauté pan. Cover with 3 cups of water, the wine, onion, carrots, parsley, peppercorns, cloves, and salt. Bring to a boil, reduce the heat, and simmer, uncovered, for about 3 minutes for a pink center. Poach a bit longer, if desired, but do not overcook. Remove the fillets from the poaching liquid with a slotted spoon and drain. Set aside, or refrigerate if serving the salmon cold.

2. Meanwhile, bring a pot of salted water to a boil, drop in the snap peas and boil, uncovered, until just tender and still bright green, 2 to 3 minutes. Drain and rinse immediately with cold water to stop the cooking.

continued

3. To make the Dill Vinaigrette, whisk the vinegar and mustard together in a small bowl. Slowly add the olive oil, whisking until emulsified. Add the dill, and salt and pepper to taste and whisk again until well combined.

4. Toss the watercress with the olive oil and divide among 4 salad plates. Place a salmon fillet over the watercress on each plate and garnish with some of the snap peas, cherry tomatoes, and olives. Drizzle with vinaigrette and serve.

chicken & soba noodle salad
with spicy asian peanut sauce

This is a very tasty salad to serve for lunch or a light dinner, and it's always a big hit with kids. The peanut sauce is also a good accompaniment to grilled vegetables, grains, and salad greens.

SERVES 6

PEANUT SAUCE:

2 TABLESPOONS PEANUT OIL

2 TEASPOONS TOASTED SESAME OIL

3 TABLESPOONS SMOOTH PEANUT BUTTER

1 1/2 TEASPOONS *SAMBAL OELEK* OR
    CHINESE CHILI PASTE (SEE NOTE)

2 TABLESPOONS LOW-SODIUM SOY SAUCE

1 TABLESPOON RICE WINE VINEGAR

SALAD:

1 PACKAGE (12 OUNCES) SOBA NOODLES

3 TABLESPOONS TOASTED SESAME OIL

2 CUPS SNOW PEAS, TRIMMED

2 CUPS COOKED CHICKEN, CHILLED
    AND CUT INTO STRIPS

3 SCALLIONS, TRIMMED AND MINCED

1/2 CUP CHOPPED FRESH FLAT-LEAF PARSLEY

1. To make the Peanut Sauce, put the peanut oil, sesame oil, peanut butter, *sambal oelek* or chili paste, soy sauce, and vinegar in a blender. Add 3 tablespoons of cold water and blend until very smooth. The sauce will keep in the refrigerator, covered, for up to 1 week.

2. To make the salad, cook the soba noodles according to the package directions. Drain, rinse with cold water, and drain again. Transfer to a large bowl and toss with the sesame oil.

3. Put the snow peas in a colander and pour boiling water over them. Rinse in cold water and drain again.

4. Add the snow peas, chicken, scallions, and parsley to the noodles and toss. Gradually add the peanut sauce and gently toss with the other salad ingredients until well combined. Serve the noodle salad chilled or at room temperature.

Note: *Sambal oelek* is available in Asian markets, health food stores, and in the international foods section of some supermarkets.

blt salad with buttermilk–blue cheese dressing

I like to make this scrumptious salad when summer tomatoes are at their peak. Although it can be made with commercial bacon, I prefer to use pancetta, which is available at gourmet shops and Italian specialty stores. Since this is a big crowd pleaser, you may want to double the recipe—after all, who doesn't love bacon?

SERVES 4 TO 6

½ CUP MAYONNAISE

1 TABLESPOON WHITE VINEGAR

1 TABLESPOON FRESH LEMON JUICE

¼ CUP WHOLE BUTTERMILK

2 TABLESPOONS CHOPPED RED ONION

2 TABLESPOONS CHOPPED FRESH
   FLAT-LEAF PARSLEY

2 TO 3 TABLESPOONS CRUMBLED BLUE CHEESE

FRESHLY GROUND BLACK PEPPER

¼ POUND BACON OR PANCETTA,
   CUT INTO ⅛-INCH SLICES

2 CUPS MIXED GREENS

2 CUPS TORN ROMAINE LETTUCE LEAVES

2 LARGE RIPE TOMATOES, CORED AND DICED

1. To make the dressing, whisk the mayonnaise, vinegar, and lemon juice together in a small bowl. Add the buttermilk and whisk again. Stir in the onion, parsley, and blue cheese. Season with pepper to taste. Taste and adjust the seasonings. The dressing will keep, covered, in the refrigerator for 1 day.

2. Fry the bacon or pancetta until crisp and drain on paper towels. When cool enough to handle, crumble and set aside.

3. Toss the greens and romaine leaves together, then place in a shallow bowl or on a platter. Arrange the tomatoes over the greens, pour over the dressing, and top with the crumbled bacon. Add a bit more fresh pepper, if desired, and serve.

fennel, orange & red onion salad

I love the licorice-tinged flavor of fennel, and it is especially good when combined with red onions and oranges. Serve this simple and refreshing salad with Thai Barbecued Chicken (page 80) or Citrus-Grilled Cornish Game Hens (page 82).

SERVES 4 TO 6

2 MEDIUM FENNEL BULBS, TRIMMED
   AND JULIENNED

1/2 MEDIUM RED ONION, THINLY SLICED

1 TABLESPOON BALSAMIC VINEGAR

2 TABLESPOONS LOW-SODIUM SOY SAUCE

2 TABLESPOONS ORANGE JUICE

1 TABLESPOON MINCED FRESH GINGER

1/3 CUP EXTRA-VIRGIN OLIVE OIL

KOSHER SALT AND FRESHLY GROUND
   BLACK PEPPER

1 MEDIUM ORANGE, PEELED, CUT INTO
   THIN ROUNDS, AND HALVED

1 TABLESPOON FRESH LEMON JUICE

1/2 CUP CHOPPED FRESH FLAT-LEAF PARSLEY

1. Put the fennel and onion in a large bowl.

2. Whisk together the vinegar, soy sauce, orange juice, ginger, and olive oil in a small bowl. Pour over the fennel and onions and toss well. Season with salt and pepper to taste. Chill the salad for 1 to 2 hours.

3. Add the oranges, lemon juice, and parsley and toss. Taste and adjust the seasonings, if necessary, and serve.

cherry tomato, basil & feta cheese salad

One of the many joys of summer cooking is that so many varieties of tomatoes and basil are widely available. It's great to make salads with a combination of cherry tomatoes—red, yellow, pear, and grape—and add a delicious mix of basil, such as sweet green, anise, and opal. This is summertime eating at its best.

SERVES 6

4 CUPS RED AND YELLOW CHERRY
 TOMATOES, HALVED

1/2 CUP MINCED SCALLIONS

1/2 CUP FRESH BASIL, THINLY SLICED

2 1/2 TABLESPOONS EXTRA-VIRGIN OLIVE OIL

I TABLESPOON BALSAMIC VINEGAR

KOSHER SALT AND FRESHLY GROUND
 BLACK PEPPER

3/4 CUP CRUMBLED FETA CHEESE
 (ABOUT 1/2 POUND)

I TABLESPOON CAPERS, DRAINED

1. Put the tomatoes, scallions, and basil in a large bowl and toss.
2. In a small bowl, whisk together 2 tablespoons of the olive oil, the vinegar, and salt and pepper to taste. Pour over the tomato mixture and toss.
3. Place the tomato mixture in a shallow bowl or on a platter. Top with the crumbled cheese and sprinkle with the capers. Drizzle with the remaining 1/2 tablespoon of olive oil. Add a bit more pepper, if desired, and serve.

radicchio, red cabbage & apple slaw

I love to create new versions of coleslaw. This one, made with shredded radicchio, red cabbage, and a Granny Smith apple, is quick and simple to prepare, and makes a spectacular presentation.

SERVES 6

½ HEAD RADICCHIO, SHREDDED (2 CUPS)

½ HEAD RED CABBAGE, SHREDDED (4 CUPS)

½ MEDIUM RED ONION, THINLY SLICED

I TEASPOON DIJON MUSTARD

2 TABLESPOONS CIDER VINEGAR

I TEASPOON SUGAR

⅓ CUP EXTRA-VIRGIN OLIVE OIL

KOSHER SALT AND FRESHLY GROUND
    BLACK PEPPER

I MEDIUM GRANNY SMITH APPLE

½ CUP CHOPPED FRESH FLAT-LEAF PARSLEY

1. Put the radicchio, cabbage, and onion in a large bowl.
2. In a small bowl, whisk the mustard, vinegar, and sugar together. Slowly add the olive oil, whisking until emulsified.
3. Pour the vinaigrette over the radicchio and cabbage mixture and toss well. Add salt and pepper to taste and toss again. Cover and chill the coleslaw in the refrigerator until ready to serve.
4. Before serving, core the apple and dice. Add the apple and parsley to the coleslaw and toss well. Taste and adjust the seasonings, if necessary, and serve.

roasted potato & green bean salad with dijon-horseradish vinaigrette

There are a couple of things to keep in mind when making this absolutely delicious roasted potato salad, the most important of which is to roast the potatoes very slowly. The slow cooking allows the garlic and olive oil time to infuse the potatoes with flavor. It's also important to mix the vinaigrette with the potatoes and green beans while they are still warm.

SERVES 6

2 POUNDS SMALL RED POTATOES, HALVED OR QUARTERED

8 CLOVES GARLIC, PEELED

3 TABLESPOONS OLIVE OIL

KOSHER SALT

1 1/2 CUPS GREEN BEANS, TRIMMED AND CUT INTO 1-INCH PIECES

DIJON-HORSERADISH VINAIGRETTE:

1 TEASPOON DIJON MUSTARD

1 TEASPOON PREPARED HORSERADISH, DRAINED

1/2 CUP EXTRA-VIRGIN OLIVE OIL

1/2 CUP CHOPPED FRESH FLAT-LEAF PARSLEY FOR GARNISH

1. Preheat the oven to 325°F.
2. Put the potatoes and garlic on a baking sheet. Add the olive oil and salt to taste and toss well to coat. Roast until the potatoes are fork-tender, about 1 1/4 to 1 1/2 hours, tossing them occasionally. Transfer them to a large bowl.
3. Shortly before the potatoes are finished, bring a medium pot of salted water to a boil. Add the beans, boil for 2 to 3 minutes, and drain. Add to the bowl with the potatoes.
4. To make the Dijon-Horseradish Vinaigrette, whisk the mustard and horseradish together in a small bowl. Slowly add the olive oil, whisking until emulsified.
5. Pour the vinaigrette over the potatoes and beans and toss well. Taste and adjust the seasonings, if necessary, garnish with parsley, and serve.

grilled sweet potatoes

I love to grill vegetables for dinner and I especially like to serve grilled sweet potatoes. Try these with barbecued chicken or grilled fish—I guarantee they'll be a big hit with your guests.

SERVES 6

2 POUNDS SWEET POTATOES

¼ CUP CORN OIL

2 TABLESPOONS LOW-SODIUM SOY SAUCE

VINAIGRETTE:

¼ CUP RICE WINE VINEGAR

¼ CUP EXTRA-VIRGIN OLIVE OIL

I TABLESPOON LOW-SODIUM SOY SAUCE

4 SCALLIONS, TRIMMED AND MINCED

2 TABLESPOONS CHOPPED FRESH FLAT-LEAF PARSLEY

I TABLESPOON CHOPPED FRESH GINGER

¼ CUP MINCED FRESH CHIVES FOR GARNISH

1. Bring a large pot of salted water to a boil and cook the potatoes until just tender, about 15 minutes. Drain and rinse under cold running water.

2. When the potatoes are cool enough to handle, peel and cut into ¼ inch slices. Put the slices on a baking sheet. In a small bowl, whisk together the corn oil and soy sauce and brush over the potatoes.

3. To make the vinaigrette, whisk together the vinegar, olive oil, and soy sauce in a small bowl. Stir in the scallions, parsley, and ginger and set aside.

4. Prepare a gas or charcoal grill. When the fire is medium-hot, and the coals are covered with a light coating of ash and glow deep red, grill the potatoes, turning them often, until just tender, about 10 minutes. If not serving immediately, put the potatoes in a warm (200°F) oven.

5. Drizzle the potatoes with the reserved vinaigrette, garnish with chives, and serve.

grilled eggplant & red peppers

These very tasty grilled eggplant and red bell peppers are delicious served with grilled lamb, or tucked into a warm baguette with a drizzle of good olive oil.

SERVES 6

1/4 CUP OLIVE OIL

I CLOVE GARLIC, THINLY SLICED

KOSHER SALT AND FRESHLY
    GROUND BLACK PEPPER

I LARGE EGGPLANT, UNPEELED, TRIMMED,
    AND SLICED INTO 1/4-INCH ROUNDS

2 LARGE RED BELL PEPPERS, STEMMED, SEEDED,
    AND QUARTERED

EXTRA-VIRGIN OLIVE OIL FOR SERVING

1. Whisk the olive oil, garlic, and salt and pepper to taste together in a small bowl. Brush the eggplant and peppers with the mixture.

2. Prepare a gas or charcoal grill. When the fire is medium-hot, and the coals are covered with a light coating of ash and glow deep red, put the eggplant on the grill and cook until golden brown, about 3 to 4 minutes per side, After about 2 minutes, add the peppers and cook until lightly charred, 2 to 3 minutes per side.

3. Drizzle the eggplant and peppers with a bit of extra-virgin olive oil and additional salt and pepper, if desired, and serve warm or at room temperature.

mixed bean salad with chive vinaigrette

I like to make this gorgeous salad and serve it with grilled chicken or fish. Although I'm partial to using red, white, and black beans in this dish, feel free to use any combination of dried beans, including black-eyed peas, flageolets, and pinto beans.

SERVES 8 TO 10

I CUP DRIED BLACK BEANS

I CUP DRIED NAVY BEANS

I CUP DRIED KIDNEY BEANS

3 CUPS CHICKEN BROTH,
    PREFERABLY HOMEMADE

3 SMALL ONIONS, PEELED

3 SMALL CARROTS, PEELED

KOSHER SALT

CHIVE VINAIGRETTE:

2 TABLESPOONS DIJON MUSTARD

1/3 CUP RED WINE VINEGAR

2 CLOVES GARLIC, MINCED

PINCH OF SUGAR

KOSHER SALT AND FRESHLY GROUND
    BLACK PEPPER

I CUP EXTRA-VIRGIN OLIVE OIL

1/3 CUP MINCED FRESH CHIVES

1/2 CUP GREEN BEANS, TRIMMED AND
    CUT INTO 1-INCH PIECES

1/2 CUP YELLOW WAX BEANS, TRIMMED AND
    CUT INTO 1-INCH PIECES

1/2 CUP CHOPPED FRESH FLAT-LEAF PARSLEY

1. Place the dried beans in 3 separate medium bowls, add water to cover by 2 inches, and let soak for 6 hours or overnight.

2. Drain the beans and cook each type separately in a medium saucepan with 1 cup of chicken broth, 1 onion, 1 carrot, salt to taste, and water to cover by 1 inch. Bring to a boil, reduce the heat, and simmer, uncovered, until the beans are tender but not mushy, 45 to 50 minutes. Drain, cool, and transfer to a large bowl.

3. Meanwhile, prepare the Chive Vinaigrette. Whisk together the mustard, vinegar, garlic, sugar, and salt and pepper to taste in a small bowl. Slowly pour in the olive oil and whisk until well blended and emulsified. Add the chives and whisk again.

continued

4. Bring a pot of salted water to a boil. Add the green and yellow wax beans and cook until just tender, 4 to 5 minutes. Drain, cool, and transfer to the bowl of cooked dried beans.
5. Toss all of the beans together. Pour the vinaigrette over them, add the parsley, and toss well to combine. Taste and adjust the seasonings, adding more salt and pepper if necessary. Serve at room temperature.

orzo, corn & chive salad

This salad makes great use of leftover cooked corn on the cob. It's lovely to serve as an accompaniment to grilled fish or lamb chops.

SERVES 6 TO 8

1 POUND ORZO

2 TABLESPOONS FRESH LEMON JUICE

1 1/2 TO 2 CUPS CORN KERNELS
   (FROM 2 COOKED FRESH EARS CORN)

1/2 CUP MINCED FRESH CHIVES

2 TABLESPOONS BALSAMIC VINEGAR

1/2 CUP EXTRA-VIRGIN OLIVE OIL

KOSHER SALT AND FRESHLY GROUND
   BLACK PEPPER

1. Bring a large pot of salted water to a boil and cook the orzo until al dente, 10 to 12 minutes. Drain well.
2. Transfer the orzo to a large bowl, drizzle the lemon juice over it, and toss well. Add the corn and chives to the orzo and toss again. Add the balsamic vinegar, olive oil, and salt and pepper to taste and toss well to combine. Taste and adjust the seasonings, if necessary.
3. Serve cold or at room temperature. Refresh the salad with a dash of lemon juice and olive oil just before serving.

fresh corn fritters

Corn fritters are wonderful served as a side dish with fried or roasted chicken. But my favorite way to serve them is the way my mother did every summer—fresh from the skillet with lots of maple syrup.

SERVES 6 TO 8; MAKES ABOUT 20 FRITTERS

3 OR 4 LARGE EARS FRESH CORN, HUSKED	I TEASPOON KOSHER SALT
3 LARGE EGGS, SEPARATED	I TEASPOON SUGAR
⅞ CUP UNBLEACHED WHITE FLOUR	PINCH OF CAYENNE PEPPER
2 TEASPOONS BAKING POWDER	CORN OIL FOR FRYING

1. Scrape the kernels from the corn cobs with a small, sharp knife. You should have 2 cups of corn. Mash ¼ cup of the corn kernels with a potato masher and transfer to a large bowl. Add the remaining corn.

2. Beat the egg yolks lightly and stir them into the corn. In a small bowl, whisk together the flour, baking powder, salt, sugar, and cayenne pepper. Add to the corn mixture and mix well to combine.

3. In a medium bowl, beat the egg whites until stiff but not dry. Gently fold them into the corn mixture.

4. Pour the oil into a large skillet to a depth of ¼ inch and heat until almost smoking. Drop the batter by tablespoons into the oil. Fry until just golden underneath, about 2 minutes. Turn and fry on the other side. When both sides are golden brown, remove with a slotted spoon and drain on paper towels. Serve at once.

desserts

lemon-glazed pound cake with fresh cherries • plum spice cake • country pear cake • key lime pie • strawberry-rhubarb pie • summer cheesecake with blueberry sauce • peach & blueberry cobbler • apple-cinnamon crisp with toasted walnuts • grilled peaches with red wine sauce • brownie sundaes with raspberry sauce • homemade fruity ice cream • lemon pudding with blackberries

summer is the time to enjoy seasonal fruits and berries. Bake them in easy-to-make cakes, pies, cobblers, and crisps, or fold farm-fresh peaches and berries into homemade ice cream.

Desserts should be kept simple, because no one wants to spend long hours baking in the kitchen. In fact, it's a good idea to do all of your baking early in the morning or in the evening when it's not too hot.

lemon-glazed pound cake with fresh cherries

This moist and delectable cake, topped with summer-fresh cherries, is a delightful treat to serve after dinner, or to savor in the afternoon with a tall glass of iced tea or coffee.

SERVES 8

½ CUP (1 STICK) UNSALTED BUTTER, AT ROOM TEMPERATURE

1½ CUPS SUGAR

3 LARGE EGGS, AT ROOM TEMPERATURE, SEPARATED

1¾ CUPS UNBLEACHED WHITE FLOUR

¼ TEASPOON BAKING SODA

⅔ CUP SOUR CREAM

1 TEASPOON VANILLA EXTRACT

1 TABLESPOON FRESH LEMON JUICE

LEMON GLAZE:

2 TO 3 TABLESPOONS CONFECTIONERS' SUGAR

JUICE OF 1 MEDIUM LEMON

1 CUP FRESH CHERRIES, HALVED AND PITTED

WHIPPED CREAM FOR SERVING (OPTIONAL)

1. Preheat the oven to 325°F. Butter and flour a 9-by-5-inch loaf pan.

2. With an electric mixer, beat the butter and sugar in a large bowl until light and fluffy. Add the egg yolks, one at a time, mixing well after each addition. Continue mixing until the batter is smooth.

3. In a shallow bowl, whisk together the flour and baking soda. Lower the speed of the mixer. Add about a third of the flour to the batter, and beat to incorporate. Add a third of the sour cream and beat again. Add the remaining flour and sour cream to the batter in alternating thirds. When the batter is smooth, stir in the vanilla and lemon juice.

continued

4. Beat the egg whites in a medium bowl until stiff peaks form. Using a rubber spatula, fold into the batter. Do not overmix the batter, but be sure to incorporate the whites thoroughly. Scrape the batter into the prepared pan and smooth the surface. Bake until the cake is golden brown, a toothpick or cake tester inserted in the center comes out clean, and the edges begin to pull away from the sides of the pan, about 1 hour and 25 minutes,

5. Let the cake cool in the pan set on a wire rack for about 15 minutes, then turn it out to cool to room temperature on the wire rack.

6. To prepare the Lemon Glaze, combine the confectioners' sugar and lemon juice in a small bowl and whisk well.

7. Place the cake on wax paper and pour the glaze over the cake, letting it run down the sides. Slice the cake and serve topped with a spoonful of cherries and whipped cream, if desired.

plum spice cake

This lovely, moist cake can be made with any kind of plum. I like to make it with ripe Italian prune plums, which are available in late summer and early fall. It's also very good with purple plums, yellow plums, or a mixture of both.

SERVES 8

2 CUPS UNBLEACHED WHITE FLOUR

1½ TEASPOONS GROUND CINNAMON

1 TEASPOON GROUND NUTMEG

½ TEASPOON GROUND CLOVES

1 TEASPOON BAKING POWDER

½ TEASPOON BAKING SODA

¾ CUP (1½ STICKS) UNSALTED BUTTER, AT ROOM TEMPERATURE

1 CUP, PLUS 1 TABLESPOON SUGAR

3 LARGE EGGS, AT ROOM TEMPERATURE

¼ CUP PLAIN NONFAT YOGURT

8 TO 12 SMALL RIPE PLUMS, HALVED AND PITTED

1. Preheat the oven to 350°F. Butter a 9-inch springform pan and set aside.

2. Whisk together the flour, 1 teaspoon of the cinnamon, nutmeg, cloves, baking powder, and baking soda in a medium bowl and set aside. In a large bowl, cream the butter and 1 cup of the sugar with an electric mixer until light and fluffy, about 5 minutes. Add the eggs, one at a time, and mix well. Reduce the speed to low, and add the flour mixture. Add the yogurt and mix again until well combined.

3. Transfer the batter to the prepared the pan and smooth the top. Arrange the plums, skin side up, in circles to cover the top. Mix the remaining 1 tablespoon of sugar and ½ teaspoon of the cinnamon together and sprinkle over the plums.

4. Bake the cake until pale golden and a toothpick or cake tester inserted in the center comes out clean, about 50 minutes. Cool to room temperature, then remove the cake from the springform pan by releasing its sides, and transfer to a plate.

country pear cake

This cake is perfect for picnics or informal parties because it's best when cut into squares and eaten out of hand. It's delicious made with fresh ripe pears, but it also works well with almost any kind of fruit or berry.

SERVES 6 TO 8

I CUP UNBLEACHED WHITE FLOUR

I TEASPOON BAKING POWDER

½ CUP (I STICK) UNSALTED BUTTER,
   AT ROOM TEMPERATURE

½ CUP LIGHT BROWN SUGAR

½ CUP, PLUS 2 TABLESPOONS
   GRANULATED SUGAR

2 LARGE EGGS, AT ROOM TEMPERATURE

2 MEDIUM PEARS, PEELED AND THINLY SLICED

½ TEASPOON GROUND CINNAMON

1. Preheat the oven to 350°F. Lightly butter and flour an 8-inch square baking pan.

2. In a medium bowl, whisk the flour and baking powder together.

3. In a large bowl, cream together the butter, brown sugar, and ½ cup of the granulated sugar with an electric mixer until light and fluffy.

4. With the mixer running and set on medium, gradually add the flour mixture to the batter. Beat in the eggs, one at a time, and mix until well combined.

5. Transfer the batter to the prepared pan and smooth the top. Arrange the pears in rows on top of the batter. Combine the remaining 2 tablespoons of granulated sugar with the cinnamon and sprinkle the mixture over the fruit. Bake until the cake begins to pull away from the sides of the pan and turns golden brown, 40 to 50 minutes. Set aside on a rack to cool.

6. When the cake is completely cool, cut it into squares and serve it fruit side up.

key lime pie

This is a very easy pie to make—the only baking required is for the crust. Be sure to keep the pie chilled until just before serving.

SERVES 6

GRAHAM CRACKER CRUST:

1 1/2 CUPS GRAHAM CRACKER CRUMBS

6 TABLESPOONS UNSALTED BUTTER, MELTED

1/4 CUP SUGAR

CUSTARD FILLING:

1/2 CUP FRESH LIME JUICE (ABOUT 4 LIMES)

1 CAN (14 OUNCES) SWEETENED
    CONDENSED MILK

2 LARGE EGG WHITES

1. Preheat the oven to 350°F. Lightly butter a 9-inch pie pan.
2. To make the crust, put the crumbs in a medium mixing bowl and add the butter and sugar. Blend well. Press the crumb mixture onto the bottom and up the sides of the pan. Smooth the bottom for an even thickness.
3. Bake the crust for 10 minutes. Remove and cool completely before filling.
4. To make the Custard Filling, mix the lime juice and the condensed milk together in a medium bowl and stir until well combined. Beat the egg whites in a small bowl until stiff peaks form and fold into the condensed milk mixture. Pour into the cooled crust and refrigerate until ready to serve.

strawberry-rhubarb pie

I love this gorgeous, summery pie. It's wonderful on its own, but even better with a scoop of whipped cream or crème fraîche.

SERVES 6

PIE DOUGH:

1¾ CUPS UNBLEACHED WHITE FLOUR

1 TEASPOON SALT

10 TABLESPOONS (1¼ STICKS)
    UNSALTED BUTTER, CHILLED AND CUT
    INTO PIECES

1 TABLESPOON VEGETABLE SHORTENING,
    CHILLED AND CUT INTO PIECES

5 TO 8 TABLESPOONS ICE WATER

PIE FILLING:

2 CUPS SLICED RHUBARB (1-INCH PIECES)

1 PINT FRESH STRAWBERRIES, HULLED
    AND HALVED

1 CUP SUGAR

2 TABLESPOONS UNBLEACHED WHITE FLOUR

1 TEASPOON VANILLA EXTRACT

1 TABLESPOON FRESH LEMON JUICE

WHIPPED CREAM OR CRÈME FRAÎCHE
    FOR SERVING

1. To make the dough, put the flour, salt, butter, and shortening into the bowl of a food processor. Pulse the food processor 4 or 5 times to break up the fat. With the motor running, add 5 tablespoons of the water. The dough should begin to mass on the blade. If not, add more water, a tablespoon at a time, as needed. When the dough holds together in a cohesive mass, it is done; do not overmix.

2. Gather the dough into a ball, and cut off about a third of it for the lattice. Flatten each piece of dough into a disk.

3. On a lightly floured surface, roll out the larger disk of dough into a circle large enough to line a 9-inch pie pan, leaving some overhang. Wrap the disks in waxed paper and refrigerate while making the filling.

4. Preheat the oven to 400°F.

5. To make the filling, in a large bowl, toss together the rhubarb, strawberries, sugar, flour, vanilla, and lemon juice. Let stand until the fruit begins to release its juices. Spoon the filling into the pie crust.

6. Roll out the other disk of dough into a 9-inch circle. Using a pizza or pastry wheel or a sharp knife, cut the dough into ¾-inch-wide strips. Arrange the strips over the top of the pie in a lattice pattern. Fold the edges of the bottom crust over the ends of the strips and flute the edges. Place the pie on a foil-lined baking sheet and place on the center rack in the oven.

7. Bake the pie for 10 minutes and reduce the heat to 350°F. Continue baking until the crust is golden brown and the pie juices are bubbling, about 45 minutes. Serve the pie with whipped cream or crème fraîche, if desired.

summer cheesecake
with blueberry sauce

This cheesecake is beautiful to look at and tastes deliciously light. Be sure that your springform pan is at least 3 inches tall because the cake will rise quite high before falling a bit. And don't open the oven to take a peek while it is baking, or it will fall too far.

SERVES 6 TO 8

GRAHAM CRACKER CRUST:

1½ CUPS GRAHAM CRACKER CRUMBS

6 TABLESPOONS UNSALTED BUTTER, MELTED

¼ CUP SUGAR

CHEESECAKE FILLING:

2 PACKAGES (½ POUND EACH) CREAM
    CHEESE, AT ROOM TEMPERATURE

½ CUP SUGAR

2 TABLESPOONS UNBLEACHED WHITE FLOUR

1 TEASPOON VANILLA EXTRACT

4 LARGE EGGS, AT ROOM TEMPERATURE,
    SEPARATED

1 CUP LIGHT CREAM

BLUEBERRY SAUCE:

1 CUP FRESH BLUEBERRIES

2 TABLESPOONS SUGAR

1 TABLESPOON FRESH LEMON JUICE

1. Preheat the oven to 350°F. Lightly butter a 9-inch springform pan.
2. To make the crust, put the crumbs in a medium bowl and add the butter and sugar. Blend well. Press the crumb mixture onto the bottom and partly up the sides of the pan. Smooth the bottom for an even thickness.
3. Bake the crust for 10 minutes. Remove and cool completely before filling.
4. Lower the oven to 325°F.
5. To make the filling, with an electric mixer, beat the cream cheese with the sugar in a large bowl until light and fluffy, 3 to 5 minutes. Add the flour and vanilla and continue beating. Mix in the egg yolks, one at a time, beating thoroughly after each addition. Add the cream and mix well.

continued

6. In a separate bowl, beat the egg whites until stiff peaks form, then gently fold them into the cream cheese mixture.

7. Pour the mixture into the prepared crust, and bake until the center is firm, about 1 hour and 15 minutes. Cool to room temperature in the pan on a rack, then chill for at least 2 hours.

8. To make the Blueberry Sauce, combine the blueberries, 2 tablespoons of water, and the sugar in a small saucepan and cook over medium heat until bubbling. Mash the berries a bit with a wooden spoon and cook for about 10 minutes more. Add the lemon juice and stir well. Cool to room temperature.

9. Remove the cheesecake from the springform pan by releasing its sides, and transfer to a plate. Spread the Blueberry Sauce over the cake, then chill before serving.

peach & blueberry cobbler

Peaches and blueberries are a luscious combination, with one fruit complementing the other perfectly in this dessert. It's best to serve the cobbler in shallow bowls, because it is very juicy.

SERVES 6

1 1/2 CUPS UNBLEACHED WHITE FLOUR

PINCH OF KOSHER SALT

7 TABLESPOONS UNSALTED BUTTER, CHILLED
    AND CUT INTO PIECES

1/4 CUP VEGETABLE SHORTENING, CHILLED
    AND CUT INTO PIECES

4 TO 5 TABLESPOONS ICE WATER

6 RIPE PEACHES, PEELED, PITTED, AND
    THINLY SLICED

1 PINT FRESH BLUEBERRIES

3 TABLESPOONS SUGAR

WHIPPED CREAM OR ICE CREAM FOR SERVING
    (OPTIONAL)

1. Preheat the oven to 450°F. Lightly butter a 7-by-9-inch baking dish.

2. Combine the flour, salt, 5 tablespoons of the butter, and the shortening in the bowl of a food processor and pulse until the mixture resembles coarse meal. Slowly add the ice water, 1 or 2 tablespoons at a time, and process until the dough begins to hold together and gather on the blade. Shape the dough into a ball, working in a little more flour if necessary. Flatten the dough into a disk, wrap in waxed paper, and refrigerate for 1 hour.

3. Put the peaches and blueberries in a large bowl. Sprinkle the sugar over the fruit and toss together. Set aside at room temperature for about 15 minutes.

4. Flour a rolling pin and on a lightly floured surface or on a piece of waxed paper, roll the dough into a rough 10-by-12-inch rectangle. Line the prepared baking dish with the dough, allowing the excess to hang over the sides. Spoon the fruit mixture evenly over the dough and dot it with the remaining 2 tablespoons of butter. Fold the overhanging dough over the fruit. (It will not cover all of the fruit.)

continued

5. Put the cobbler on the center rack of the oven and immediately reduce the temperature to 425°F. Bake until the crust is golden and the fruit is bubbling, 30 to 35 minutes.

6. Spoon the cobbler, either warm or at room temperature, into shallow bowls. Serve with whipped cream or ice cream, if desired.

apple-cinnamon crisp with toasted walnuts

Here is a wonderful, simple dessert to make during apple season. I like to make this crisp with a tart apple, such as Granny Smith, Macoun, or Northern Spy.

SERVES 6

FILLING:

6 TART RED OR GREEN APPLES, PEELED, CORED, AND COARSELY CHOPPED

1/2 CUP SUGAR

1 TABLESPOON FRESH LEMON JUICE

1 TEASPOON GROUND CINNAMON

1/2 TEASPOON GROUND CLOVES

1/2 TEASPOON GROUND NUTMEG

3/4 CUP WALNUT HALVES, LIGHTLY TOASTED (SEE NOTE)

2 TABLESPOONS APPLE CIDER OR APPLE JUICE

TOPPING:

1/2 CUP UNBLEACHED WHITE FLOUR

1/2 CUP SUGAR

4 TABLESPOONS UNSALTED BUTTER, CHILLED AND CUT INTO PIECES

ICE CREAM OR WHIPPED CREAM FOR SERVING (OPTIONAL)

1. Preheat the oven to 350°F.
2. To make the filling, in a large bowl, combine the apples, sugar, lemon juice, cinnamon, cloves, nutmeg, and walnuts and toss to mix. Transfer to a 12-by-8-by-2-inch baking dish and sprinkle the cider or juice over the fruit.
3. To make the topping, whisk together the flour and sugar in a medium bowl. Using your fingers or a pastry blender, cut the butter into the flour mixture, working it until the mixture is crumbly. Sprinkle evenly over the fruit. Bake the apple crisp until the topping is lightly browned and the fruit is bubbling, 40 to 50 minutes, Serve warm, topped with ice cream or whipped cream, if desired.

Note: To toast the walnuts, spread them on a baking sheet and toast them in a 350°F oven or toaster oven until golden brown and fragrant, about 5 minutes. Shake the pan once or twice for even toasting. Slide the nuts off the baking sheet as soon as they reach the desired color to halt the cooking. Let cool.

grilled peaches with red wine sauce

Fresh peaches are a wonderful thing to cook on the grill after the fire has died down a bit. They don't require a lot of time or attention, just a bit of basting with a sauce of red wine and brown sugar. They're delicious hot off the grill with a scoop of vanilla or cinnamon ice cream.

SERVES 6

4 LARGE RIPE PEACHES, PITTED AND HALVED

CORN OIL FOR BRUSHING

2 CUPS FRUITY RED WINE,
    SUCH AS ZINFANDEL OR BEAUJOLAIS

2 TABLESPOONS BROWN SUGAR

VANILLA OR CINNAMON ICE CREAM
    FOR SERVING

1. Prepare a gas or charcoal grill and let the coals die down until the fire is medium-low.
2. Brush the peaches with corn oil. Whisk the wine and sugar together until well combined.
3. Place the peaches on the grill, cut side down, cook about 3 minutes, and turn. Brush with the red wine mixture and continue cooking until fork-tender, 20 to 25 minutes, turning and basting often.
4. To serve, spoon a bit of the wine sauce into each shallow bowl, add a grilled peach half, drizzle with a bit more sauce, and serve with a scoop of ice cream.

brownie sundaes with raspberry sauce

Here's a terrific dessert to serve after a light dinner. Your guests will rave.

SERVES 6

5 OUNCES GOOD-QUALITY
   UNSWEETENED CHOCOLATE

1/2 CUP (1 STICK) UNSALTED BUTTER,
   AT ROOM TEMPERATURE

1 1/4 CUPS SUGAR

1/2 TEASPOON VANILLA EXTRACT

3 LARGE EGGS, AT ROOM TEMPERATURE

3/4 CUP UNBLEACHED WHITE FLOUR

1/2 CUP WALNUTS, CHOPPED (OPTIONAL)

RASPBERRY SAUCE:

1 CUP FRESH RASPBERRIES

1/4 CUP SUGAR

1 1/2 TEASPOONS FRESH LEMON JUICE

VANILLA ICE CREAM FOR SERVING

1. Preheat the oven to 325°F. Butter and flour an 8-inch square baking pan.

2. Melt the chocolate and butter in the top of a double boiler over simmering water. Remove from the heat and let cool.

3. Put the sugar in a medium bowl and stir in the chocolate mixture. Mix with an electric mixer until well blended and smooth. Scrape down the inside of the bowl with a spatula.

4. With the mixer on low, add the vanilla to the chocolate mixture and then the eggs, one at a time. Beat until the eggs are well incorporated, scrape down the bowl, and beat again until the mixture is very smooth. Add the flour to the chocolate mixture and mix well by hand. Stir in the walnuts, if using.

5. Transfer the batter to the prepared pan and spread evenly. Place on the center oven rack and bake until a thin crust forms on the top and a toothpick or cake tester inserted in the middle comes out clean, about 35 minutes. Cool in the pan on a rack for 1 hour. Cut into squares.

6. To make the Raspberry Sauce, put the raspberries and sugar in a small saucepan and heat, stirring frequently, to a boil. Reduce the heat to low and mash the raspberries with the back of a wooden spoon. Continue cooking until the berries are cooked down into a sauce, 10 to 15 minutes. Cool and strain through a sieve. Return the sauce to the pan and stir in the lemon juice. Taste and add more lemon juice or sugar if necessary.

7. To serve the sundaes, spoon a bit of the sauce in the bottom of a bowl and place a brownie over it. Add a scoop of the ice cream and spoon more raspberry sauce over the top.

homemade fruity ice cream

If you have never tried making homemade ice cream, don't wait any longer. It's really easy to do with a commercial ice-cream maker, and you won't be disappointed with the results. In fact, it will be hard to resist eating the partially frozen ice cream right out of the machine's cannister. You can use almost any fruit in this recipe—peaches, nectarines, strawberries, blueberries, raspberries—the possibilities are endless.

SERVES 6; MAKES 1 QUART

1⅓ CUPS HEAVY (WHIPPING) CREAM, CHILLED

⅔ CUP HALF-AND-HALF, CHILLED

⅔ CUP SUGAR

1 TEASPOON VANILLA EXTRACT

1½ CUPS COARSELY MASHED FRESH PEELED PEACHES OR NECTARINES, OR STRAWBERRIES, BLUEBERRIES, OR RASPBERRIES, CHILLED

1 TABLESPOON FRESH LEMON JUICE

1. In a large bowl, stir together the cream and half-and-half. Add the sugar and vanilla and stir until the sugar dissolves.

2. Toss the fruit with the lemon juice in a small bowl.

3. Transfer the cream mixture to the chilled cannister of an ice-cream machine and freeze according to the manufacturer's instructions. When the ice cream is nearly frozen, add the fruit and churn until frozen. (It will be softer than commercial ice cream.) Transfer to a 1-quart metal or plastic container and freeze until the mixture is firm and the flavors have had time to blend, at least 2 to 3 hours.

lemon pudding with blackberries

Chilled lemon pudding served with fresh blackberries makes a lovely, warm-weather dessert. If blackberries are not available, you can use fresh strawberries or blueberries. For the best flavor and texture, serve the pudding on the same day it is made.

SERVES 6

1/4 CUP CORNSTARCH

2 1/2 CUPS WHOLE MILK

3 LARGE EGG YOLKS

I CUP SUGAR

2 TEASPOONS GRATED LEMON ZEST

PINCH OF KOSHER SALT

1/2 CUP FRESH LEMON JUICE

I TABLESPOON VANILLA EXTRACT

1/2 CUP HEAVY (WHIPPING) CREAM

2 CUPS FRESH BLACKBERRIES,
    SLICED STRAWBERRIES, OR BLUEBERRIES

WHIPPED CREAM FOR GARNISH (OPTIONAL)

1. In a medium saucepan, combine the cornstarch and 1/3 cup of the milk and whisk until smooth. Add the egg yolks, sugar, I teaspoon of the zest, and the salt and whisk again. Stir in the remaining milk and cook over medium-low heat, whisking constantly, until heated through, 4 to 6 minutes. Raise the heat to medium-high and cook, whisking constantly, until the mixture is boiling and smooth, 3 to 5 minutes. It may thicken and then thin out a bit.

2. Strain the pudding mixture through a fine-mesh sieve into a medium bowl. Stir in the remaining zest and the lemon juice and set the bowl over a larger bowl filled with ice cubes and cold water. Let the pudding cool, stirring occasionally, until it starts to thicken, about 5 minutes. Stir in the vanilla.

3. With an electric mixer set on high speed, whip the cream until soft peaks form and fold into the pudding mixture. Spoon into six 6-ounce custard cups or ramekins, cover with plastic wrap, and chill for at least I hour before serving. Top with the berries and whipped cream, if desired.

beach house drinks

campari & blood orange juice cocktails •
beach house cosmos • vodka, lemonade &
mint coolers • white rum & lime sea breezes •
sparkling lemonade with fresh raspberries •
iced orange & ginger tea • iced mint tea •
iced mocha-cinnamon coffee

it's easy to pour a beer or mix a vodka and tonic for friends dropping by for a drink, but why not make cocktail hour or party time at the beach a little more interesting? Whip up a big pitcher of Beach House Cosmos or serve elegant Campari cocktails made with freshly squeezed blood oranges. Festive thirst-quenchers like these are just the right thing for summertime sipping.

It's also a great time to make cooling lemonade and iced tea and coffee from scratch. These delicious and refreshing drinks are so enjoyable to sip while relaxing in a hammock or gazing at the waves from a beach chair.

campari & blood orange juice cocktails

Bittersweet Campari, mixed with freshly squeezed blood orange juice and a splash of club soda over ice, makes an elegant summertime drink to sip on a warm afternoon. If blood oranges aren't available, use navel oranges.

SERVES 2

1/2 CUP CAMPARI

1 CUP FRESH BLOOD ORANGE JUICE

2 SPLASHES OF CLUB SODA OR SELTZER

2 ORANGE SLICES FOR GARNISH

Pour 1/4 cup of the Campari into each of 2 ice-filled glasses. Add 1/2 cup of the orange juice and a splash of club soda or seltzer to each glass and stir. Serve garnished with an orange slice.

beach house cosmos

Cosmos are a very popular party drink, but one drawback to making a lot of them is the time spent squeezing so many fresh limes. A caterer friend of mine gave me this tip for making big pitchers of cosmos for a crowd—use frozen limeade instead. Very tasty!

SERVES 12 TO 14

4 CUPS LIMEADE, MADE FROM CONCENTRATE

1 CUP CRANBERRY JUICE

2 CUPS VODKA

$\frac{1}{2}$ CUP TRIPLE SEC

12 TO 14 LIME SLICES FOR GARNISH

Pour the limeade, cranberry juice, vodka, and Triple Sec into a container and shake. Chill thoroughly. Before serving shake again, then transfer to a large glass pitcher. Serve in martini glasses garnished with lime slices.

vodka, lemonade & mint coolers

Try this incredibly refreshing drink on a warm summer evening. It's delicious when made with commercial pink or yellow lemonade, but for something really special, try it with Sparkling Lemonade with Fresh Raspberries (page 147).

SERVES 6

4 CUPS LEMONADE

1 CUP VODKA

¼ CUP CHOPPED FRESH MINT

6 LEMON SLICES FOR GARNISH

6 MINT LEAVES FOR GARNISH

Pour the lemonade and vodka into a large pitcher, add the mint and stir well. To serve, pour into ice-filled tall glasses and garnish with lemon slices and mint leaves.

white rum & lime sea breezes

Sea breezes are best known as vodka drinks, but they're also mighty good with white rum and lots of fresh lime.

SERVES 6

3 CUPS CRANBERRY JUICE

⅔ CUP GRAPEFRUIT JUICE

JUICE OF 1 LIME

1 CUP WHITE RUM

6 LIME SLICES FOR GARNISH

Pour the cranberry juice, grapefruit juice, lime juice, and rum into a large pitcher and stir well. Serve over ice in highball glasses, garnished with lime slices.

sparkling lemonade with fresh raspberries

Lemonade made from fresh lemons is delightfully refreshing to sip and enjoy all summer. You will need some Sugar Syrup, which is basically 2 parts sugar to 1 part water. It's an excellent idea to keep a containerful in the refrigerator for adding to lemonade, iced tea, and other summer drinks.

SERVES 6

½ CUP FRESH LEMON JUICE (2 TO 3 LEMONS)

½ CUP SUGAR SYRUP (RECIPE FOLLOWS)

6 SPLASHES OF CLUB SODA OR SELTZER

1 CUP FRESH RASPBERRIES

6 LEMON SLICES FOR GARNISH

1. In a large pitcher, combine the lemon juice, Sugar Syrup, and 1 quart of cold water and mix well. Chill in the refrigerator for at least 1 hour.

2. Pour the lemonade over ice-filled glasses, add a splash of club soda or seltzer to each and stir. Garnish each glass with a few raspberries and a lemon slice.

sugar syrup

MAKES ABOUT 2½ CUPS

4 CUPS SUGAR

In a heavy saucepan, bring the sugar and 2 cups of water to a boil over medium-high heat. Boil for 2 to 3 minutes, stirring to dissolve the sugar completely. Remove from the heat, let cool, and refrigerate in a covered container. The syrup will keep for up to 3 weeks.

iced orange & ginger tea

Nothing is more refreshing than homemade iced tea made with orange pekoe leaves and fresh ginger.

SERVES 6

3 TABLESPOONS ORANGE PEKOE TEA LEAVES

½ CUP SUGAR

2 TABLESPOONS SLICED FRESH GINGER

I CINNAMON STICK

6 ORANGE SLICES FOR GARNISH

1. Bring 2 quarts of water to a full boil in a large saucepan. Add the tea, sugar, ginger, and cinnamon stick and remove the pan from the heat. Cover and let stand for 5 minutes. Stir gently to make sure that the sugar is dissolved. Let stand for 5 minutes longer.
2. Strain the tea into a pitcher and let cool to room temperature. Refrigerate for at least 2 hours. Serve over ice in chilled glasses, garnished with the orange slices.

iced mint tea

I like to make a big pitcher of iced tea flavored with fresh mint to have on hand in the refrigerator. Savoring a tall glass of it on a lazy afternoon is what summer is all about.

SERVES 6

3 TABLESPOONS MINT TEA LEAVES

2 TABLESPOONS FRESH MINT LEAVES

2 TABLESPOONS HONEY

6 LEMON SLICES FOR GARNISH

1. Bring 2 quarts of water to a full boil in a large saucepan. Add the tea and mint leaves, and remove the pan from the heat. Cover and let stand for 5 minutes. Add the honey and stir until dissolved.
2. Strain the tea into a pitcher and let cool to room temperature. Refrigerate for at least 2 hours. Serve over ice in chilled glasses, garnished with the lemon slices.

iced mocha-cinnamon coffee

Here's a warm-weather treat to serve to your guests after lunch or dinner.

SERVES 6

6 CUPS STRONG, FRESHLY BREWED COFFEE

6 OUNCES UNSWEETENED CHOCOLATE

1 CINNAMON STICK

1/4 TO 1/2 CUP SUGAR SYRUP (PAGE 147)

CREAM OR MILK FOR SERVING

1. Pour the coffee into a large saucepan. Melt the chocolate with the cinnamon stick in a double boiler over boiling water. Add to the coffee and stir well.

2. Strain the drink into a large pitcher, discarding the cinnamon stick. Add 1/4 cup of the Sugar Syrup and stir well. Taste and adjust to desired sweetness. Let cool to room temperature and refrigerate for at least 2 hours. Serve over ice in chilled glasses, with cream or milk.

acknowledgments

My thanks and gratitude go to:
Leslie Jonath, my editor at Chronicle Books, and her associates, Laurel
Mainard and Kevin Toyama, for all of their help, support, and good humor.

Vanessa Dina, also at Chronicle, who was delightful to work with on the
design of this book.

Angela Miller, my agent, who helped make this book happen.

Rita Maas, for her wonderful photography, and Roscoe Betsill, for his
beautiful food styling. They both captured the spirit of the food perfectly.

Barbara Fritz, for prop styling, and to Anthropologie and Crate & Barrel,
for the use of their wares in some of the photographs.

The good people at Gosman's Fish Market in Montauk, N.Y., and the great,
knowledgeable crew at Mt. Kisco Seafood for providing the best seafood
imagineable for recipe testing.

My friends and family, all gracious and gregarious dinner guests, with whom
I have shared good food and great times for many years.

index

TABLE OF EQUIVALENTS

The exact equivalents in the following tables have been rounded for convenience.

LIQUID/DRY MEASURES

U.S.	Metric
¼ teaspoon	1.25 milliliters
½ teaspoon	2.5 milliliters
1 teaspoon	5 milliliters
1 tablespoon (3 teaspoons)	15 milliliters
1 fluid ounce (2 tablespoons)	30 milliliters
¼ cup	60 milliliters
⅓ cup	80 milliliters
½ cup	120 milliliters
1 cup	240 milliliters
1 pint (2 cups)	480 milliliters
1 quart (4 cups, 32 ounces)	960 milliliters
1 gallon (4 quarts)	3.84 liters
1 ounce (by weight)	28 grams
1 pound	454 grams
2.2 pounds	1 kilogram

OVEN TEMPERATURE

Fahrenheit	Celsius	Gas
250	120	½
275	140	1
300	150	2
325	160	3
350	180	4
375	190	5
400	200	6
425	220	7
450	230	8
475	240	9
500	260	10

LENGTH

U.S.	Metric
⅛ inch	3 millimeters
¼ inch	6 millimeters
½ inch	12 millimeters
1 inch	2.5 centimeters